Breaking Through the Stained Glass Ceiling

Breaking Through the Stained Glass Ceiling

Women Pastoring Large Churches

HiRho Park and Susan Willhauck, Editors

General Board of Higher Education and Ministry
The United Methodist Church
Nashville, Tennessee

The General Board of Higher Education and Ministry leads and serves The United Methodist Church in the recruitment, preparation, nurture, education, and support of Christian leaders—lay and clergy—for the work of making disciples of Jesus Christ for the transformation of the world. Its vision is that a new generation of Christian leaders will commit boldly to Jesus Christ and be characterized by intellectual excellence, moral integrity, spiritual courage, and holiness of heart and life.

The General Board of Higher Education and Ministry of The United Methodist Church is the church's agency for educational, institutional, and ministerial leadership. It serves as an advocate for the intellectual life of the church. The Board's mission embodies the Wesleyan tradition of commitment to the education of laypersons and ordained persons by providing access to higher education for all persons.

ISBN 978-0-938162-64-3

Produced by the Office of Interpretation
Manufactured in the United States of America

Contents

ACKNOWLEDGMENTS

We are deeply grateful to all of the lead women pastors of The United Methodist Church who participated in the Lead Women Pastors Project (LWPP) and agreed to be interviewed, surveyed, and observed to help further the church's knowledge and appreciation for the ministries of clergywomen. (For this book, the term *lead women pastors* applies to those female pastors who are serving churches with memberships of 1,000 or more.) They gave of their time to attend and help lead gatherings, to participate in online discussions, and to coach younger clergywomen. This project modeled a courageous, collaborative, and creative spirit, which we do not take for granted, and we give our profound thanks.

We also are thankful to the women bishops who contributed to the project: Deborah Kiesey, Violet Fisher (ret.), Debra Wallace Padgett, and others who offered their encouragement. Our thanks goes to Wesley Theological Seminary, which hosted the online portion of the study; and to the Lewis Center for Church Leadership at Wesley, which provided research analysis on our survey. Thank you also to Dr. Laceye Warner, executive vice dean and associate professor of the practice of evangelism and Methodist studies at Duke Divinity School, who spoke at a LWPP gathering, offering a scholarly and humorous view of the great cloud of witnesses of women ministers in early Methodism. We are especially grateful to Dr. Elisabeth Schüssler-Fiorenza, Krister Stendahl professor of divinity at Harvard Divinity School, who gave the keynote address on "Ekklesia of Women" at our 2011 lead women pastors' retreat. Dr. Schüssler-Fiorenza's renowned work in feminist biblical interpretation has been an inspiration to many clergywomen everywhere.

The Office of Interpretation of the General Board of Higher

Education and Ministry (GBHEM) was instrumental in the publication of this project; specifically we acknowledge Terri Hiers, executive director, Vicki Brown, associate editor/writer, and Donnie Reed, graphic designer. We are excited that under their guidance this work initially was published as an e-book, a new wave in church publishing that promotes sustainability and accessibility to a wide audience. We owe our gratitude to Dr. Kim Cape, the first woman general secretary of the General Board of Higher Education and Ministry, who broke a glass ceiling herself and shared the spirit of this project and encouraged us to publish this work. It has been our joy to work with such bold, dynamic, and faithful women leaders. We also appreciate Renée Chavez, the managing editor, and Joshua Hestand, coordinator of the Clergy Lifelong Learning office at GBHEM.

FOREWORD

Elisabeth Schüssler Fiorenza
Harvard University Divinity School

The Federal Glass Ceiling Commission has defined the metaphor of "glass ceiling" as "the unseen, yet unbreachable barrier that keeps minorities and women from rising to the upper rungs of the corporate ladder, regardless of their qualifications or achievements."[1] In the intervening years since the report was published, wo/men have cracked the "glass ceilings" in business, politics, or the academy.

This book, *Breaking Through the Stained Glass Ceiling: Women Pastoring Large Churches*, edited by Rev. Dr. HiRho Y. Park and Dr. Susan Willhauck and sponsored by the General Board of Higher Education and Ministry of The United Methodist Church, carefully documents how difficult it is still for clergy-wo/men[2] to shatter the "stained" glass ceiling of the church too. When the project began in 2008, there were 64 *lead wo/men pastors* serving parishes with more than 1,000 members. In the fall of 2011, there were 94 wo/men in such leadership positions.

The book amply documents how these wo/men have changed the style of preaching and ministry, tells of their struggles to combine work and family, discusses conflict and resource management, and explores spirituality and the process of coaching wo/men for such leadership positions. However, it also notes that there is still only one "minority" wo/man in the position of lead pastor serving one of the top one hundred largest United Methodist churches (see the introduction). Hence, it seems to me that the "glass" ceiling metaphor is best understood as a "class" ceiling which in society and church allows breakthroughs for highly educated white and upper class wo/men, but not for the majority of wo/men. Why does the ceiling still hold in society and church, despite the many successful attempts at cracking it? The answer is *kyriarchy*.[3]

Western democracy as well as Christian churches proclaim the equality of all citizens or of all the baptized. However, it has taken centuries of struggle for wo/men to receive full citizen status in society and churches, and many wo/men have still not achieved it. Like Western democracies, so also Christian churches have their historical roots in antiquity. Western democracy harks back to ancient Greece, where freeborn wo/men, slave wo/men, and Barbarian wo/men were excluded from citizenship and participation in the *ekklésia*, the decision-making democratic assembly. This kyriarchal democratic "glass/class ceiling" is part of the legacy of Athenian democracy whose structures were taken over by modern Western democracies. The emancipation movements of the last three or more centuries have therefore struggled against kyriarchally determined inequality and for full citizenship.

As far as we can still see, Christian communities were formed in the first centuries CE as *ekklésiai*, as radical democratic assemblies, which were not kyriarchally structured but whose members were all equal because they all had received G*d's Spirit: There was neither Jew nor Greek, slave nor free, or male and female (Gal. 3:28). However, very soon a kyriarchal imperial glass ceiling was constructed in order to adapt the small Christian ekklésiai to their surrounding society in the Roman empire. It is debated among scholars whether these attempts by the Roman kyriarchal ethos are already found in the genuine Pauline letters or only toward the end of the first century. In any case, it must not be overlooked that these scriptural texts are prescriptive texts that seek to change the radical equality of the Spirit-filled ekklésiai in order to adapt the Christian communities to their surrounding kyriarchal societies.

Today, the opposite process seems to be in order. The more egalitarian a democratic society becomes, the more the different Christian churches are called to return to their ekklésial roots of radical equality in the Spirit. Rather than to defend kyriarchal structures of inequality, Christian churches are called to engender and support radical egalitarian societal structures not only of gender, but also of race, class, age, or immigration.

Wo/men who seek to crack the various societal and religious glass ceilings are therefore in the vanguard of these struggles for radical equality, if they do not forget that wo/men are not the same. We are not only gendered but also raced, classed, nationalized, and colonialized. Wo/men do not have an essence in common, but we share cultural kyriarchal gender socializations that are different but also often similar in a globalized world. The editors of and contributors to *Breaking Through the Stained Glass Ceiling* are well aware of this. They realized early on that wo/men have internalized cultural kyriarchal stereotypes that prevent us from reaching our full potential of leadership. Hence, they have developed a coaching process that enables wo/men in leadership to work together to envision and enact church as the ekklésia of wo/men, as a discipleship community.

Notes

1. Federal Glass Ceiling Commission, *Solid Investments: Making Full Use of the Nation's Human Capital* (Washington, D.C.: U.S. Department of Labor, November 1995), 4.
2. In order to lift into consciousness the linguistic violence of so-called generic male-centered language, I write the term *wo/men* with a slash. I do so in order to use the term "wo/men" and not "men" in an inclusive way. I suggest that whenever you read "wo/men," you need to understand it in the generic sense. Wo/man includes man, she includes he, and female includes male. Feminist studies of language have elaborated that Western, kyriocentric—that is, master, lord, father, male-centered language systems—understand language as both generic and as gender specific. Wo/men always must think at least twice, if not three times, and adjudicate whether we are meant or not by so-called generic terms such as "men," "humans," "Americans," or "pastors." To use "wo/men" as an inclusive generic term invites male readers to learn how to "think twice" and to experience what it means not to be addressed explicitly. Since wo/men always must arbitrate whether we are meant or not, I consider it a good spiritual exercise for men to acquire the same sophistication and to learn how to engage in the same hermeneutical process of "thinking twice" and of asking whether they are meant when I speak of wo/men. Since, according to the philosopher Wittgenstein, the limits of our language are the limits of our world, such a change of language patterns is a very important step toward the realization of a new feminist consciousness.
3. Derived from *kyrios* = lord, slavemaster, father, husband, elite propertied gentleman and *archein* = domination.

Introduction from the Editors:
Cracks in the Stained Glass Ceiling

HiRho Park and Susan Willhauck

This is a book about, for, and by women who pastor large churches (those of more than a thousand members) and for those who want to learn about this remaining frontier for women's leadership in the church. Women have made lots of gains in church leadership in our lifetime. Right now, more than half of the students in seminary are women.[1] Women have made and will continue to make a huge impact on the church. The elephant in the room remains: there is still blatant sexism in the ways people respond to women's leadership. Although we are in an era where many perceive women in ministry to be normal, many churches still simply do not want a woman pastor. Some of these even vocalize that sentiment openly, without embarrassment or accountability. For others such a mindset is unspoken but very much present.

Despite these challenges, these women pastors, whose voices you will hear within this book, overwhelmingly believe that serving a large church is their distinctive call, and they are gracefully and uniquely fulfilling that call and continuing to transform the church. A United Methodist bishop, Jane Allen Middleton of the Central Pennsylvania Conference, talked about women's leadership in a recent interview. She said, "We aren't just men in skirts. We have our own styles, we have another way of looking at the world, and we have changed the church."[2] We feel that "not men in skirts" succinctly captures a conviction that we no longer operate on a male paradigm of leadership.

We are honored to serve as editors of this book on women in large churches and what differences their leadership makes for the church. We are HiRho Park, director of Clergy Lifelong Learning of the General Board of Higher Education and Ministry of The United Methodist Church, an ordained elder; and Susan Will-hauck, associate professor of pastoral theology at Atlantic School of Theology and a licensed local pastor in the UMC. But the voices you will hear within are those of lead women pastors of large churches. (See the list of contributors at the end of this book.)

While this book comes from a United Methodist context, we believe that it will be useful and applicable not only to the church but also to institutions still struggling to accept and affirm women's leadership. We believe that creative connections between women will transform leadership, so we have included questions at the end of each chapter, and we invite you to join in circle dialogues with other women leaders to read this book together and reflect on the questions and learn from each other.

We are aware that some people, including many in institutional leadership, think women's battles have been won, at least in the United States, and who point out that women pastors are nothing new and see no need for a book on women's leadership now. And it is true that women entering seminary these days have women leaders as role models and so do not lack confidence in their ability to lead the church. But strength in numbers does not mean women will not face discrimination and prejudice and barriers in their leadership roles. In Canada, where there are more women in ministry than men, women clergy lament the recurring sexism that is destructive to their well-being and to the church. One clergywoman in the United States shared this story of her ordination interview with us:

> The questions I received from the interview committee kind of shocked me because we were in the last decade of the twentieth century. One male clergy asked me why I was trying to get ordained ahead of my husband, who started the ordination process later than me. Another male clergy on the committee stated that I was lucky to have a baby before my ordination (I just had a baby at the time of the inter-

view), since if I was still pregnant for my ordination ceremony, there would be questions about ordaining the fetus
through me.

While we do not subscribe to the "woman for the sake of a
woman" tokenism, we believe that it is just as important as ever to
celebrate and advocate for the achievements and the "firsts" of
women in society. Consider Sarah Attar, the first Saudi Arabian
woman ever to run in the Olympics (2012); Marissa Mayer, first
woman to lead Google at age thirty-seven; or Park Geun-hye, the
first woman to become the presidential candidate of a major political party in South Korea (where the culture is inculcated with
patriarchy) and elected as the first woman president. And don't forget Joaquina Filipe Nhanala, the first African woman elected to the
United Methodist episcopacy in 2008; and Ellen Johnson Sirleaf,
the first woman president of Liberia. Even if you do not agree with
the politics of certain female politicians, it is a good thing that
women are major players on the political front. That the dubious
honor that the first women invited to join the Augusta National
Golf Club didn't happen until 2012 may go against all you believe
about classism and exclusivism, it does suggest that even the last
standing male-only bastions are crumbling and can no longer jus-
tify sexist policies.

Just as some dismiss racial differences with claims to "color-
blindness," some may hold the view that since women's ministry is
normal, we can and ought to be "gender-blind" in the church. But
we are a gendered people, whether socially constructed or something deeper. We who do ministry as women can affirm our gender
up front as a part of how we preach, teach, provide pastoral care,
and lead, perhaps as male clergy who have asserted their own gender from the pulpit since time eternal. The authors of *Women,
Spirituality, and Transformational Leadership* say that many organizations that women have recently entered are "structured in
traditional 'masculine' ways using hierarchical leadership models
and processes that may not invite the deepest feminine wisdom or
effectively catalyze social change."[3] As the Rev. Trudy Robinson

said, "I worry about our trying to fit into a box that has been defined by men."

Typically the church with a large membership has been viewed as the benchmark for judging ministerial success in mainline denominations. And, as such, it has remained essentially an intact stained glass ceiling for clergywomen, until a few women began to crack it. We do not make the presumption that bigger is always better or that women ought to "climb the ladder" to that benchmark of success, but aim to ensure that all ministries are fully open to women's leadership and that women's leadership is valued in all settings. This project seeks to tap into the rich resource of lead women pastors to better understand pastoral leadership. Rather than measuring pastoral effectiveness against already established criteria that are male defined, we look at ways lead women pastors are redefining pastoral effectiveness on their own terms. People who are invested in male models of leadership (especially for the large church) are loath to admit that women bring anything unique to leadership or the ability to reform the church, because that threatens the status quo of males in charge. We made no essentialist assumptions, however, in our grounded research methodology, but sought to discover the content and future direction of women's leadership in the large church setting.

Lead women pastors have been cracking a glass ceiling within the church in spite of an apparent lack of support, affirmation, and recognition of their unique contributions. As one clergywoman put it, "The ceilings are at different heights and they keep resetting them." Ramming up against a glass ceiling is a dangerous activity, and many women have the concussions to prove it. But if it weren't for the wounds of many, where would we be?

At the end of the 2008 Democratic primary race, Hillary Rodham Clinton conceded to her opponent and bid farewell to her supporters with these words: "Although we weren't able to shatter that highest, hardest glass ceiling this time, thanks to you, it's got about 18 million cracks in it, . . . And the light is shining through like never before, filling us all with the hope and the sure knowledge that the path will be a little easier next time."[4]

Of course, Clinton has gone on to distinguished service as secretary of state, the third woman in the United States to hold this position, with many diplomatic achievements.

In *Women and Leadership: The State of Play and Strategies for Change*, Barbara Kellerman and Deborah Rhode acknowledge that despite a half century of equal-opportunity legislation, women are still frustratingly underrepresented in leadership roles in society. Though the situation has improved over time, women are still a small minority in the most influential leadership positions. They cite gender bias, double standards, and disproportionate family responsibilities among the obstacles to leadership opportunities for women. "The 'great man' model of leadership is still with us."[5] Keeping women out of influential leadership roles compromises fundamental principles of equal opportunity and social justice. They also note that researchers consistently find a positive correlation between a high representation of women leaders and business success. Though correlation does not always imply causation, they argue that there are "strong reasons to believe that diversity in leadership has tangible pay-offs."[6]

Clergywomen and proponents of women's leadership in the church can continue to uphold and claim the gifts of women for the church despite the barriers. Transformation of any kind can only come from a holy scuffle. Women in ministry in our tradition have been engaged in a graceful struggle, one of those genuine paradoxes of leadership. Struggle implies suffering, great effort, and determination; perhaps even the gnashing of teeth, flailing of arms, and butting of heads. Yet a struggle can also be a dance with movements that free us from past confines. When that struggle is grace-filled, it is one in which God is made known, wisdom prevails, and metamorphosis happens.

Several studies revealed that women clergy were not faring very well in many settings and were leaving the ministry (more than their male counterparts).[7] Salary studies showed a wide discrepancy between equally qualified and experienced male and female clergy. The most recent salary study within the UMC proved that male pastors receive 13 percent more salary than female pastors.[8]

Although some women have assumed positions of authority as bishops, moderators, superintendents, etc., in many denominations that ordain women, the topic of women serving large churches is still a contentious matter. Who are they? Where are they? How are they doing? In the early 1990s just 5 percent of the senior pastors of Protestant churches were female, according to the Barna Research Group. But that figure doubled to 10 percent by 2009.[9] Although the percentage was still small, people wanted to know more about these few pioneering female leaders.

Because this book is birthed by a particular study of these women clergy within The United Methodist Church called the Lead Women's Pastors Project (LWPP), it will be helpful to provide some background on this project in the story of the graceful struggle of United Methodist clergywomen. In 2006 the International Clergywomen's Consultation was held in Chicago to celebrate the fiftieth anniversary of clergy rights for women in the Methodist tradition.[10] That event fueled more interest in how women were cracking the stained glass ceiling to serve in large membership churches. As The United Methodist Church greets a new era of women's leadership, a question that arose was, "How can the Church equip younger generations of clergywomen to fulfill their calling to serve the needs of the present age that necessitates gender inclusivity in theology and practice?" Thus the Lead Women Pastors Project was launched in 2008 by the General Board of Higher Education and Ministry and continues today. The collaborative leadership team also included the Rev. Patricia Farris and the Rev. Trudy Robinson. They have written a reflection and epilogue for this book.

All United Methodist clergywomen serving at that time as lead pastors of large churches were invited to participate in the study.[11] The project quickly attracted the attention of other denominations and the national and international media. An Associated Press article appeared in dozens of newspapers including *USA Today,* and another article was published in the *Christian Century*; we had interviews on YouTube, and in many other online and print publications. The experiences of these lead women pastors will serve as a resource for the formation of future generations of women's leadership.

The goals of the LWPP include: (1) establishing an online continuing education and support network for clergywomen serving as lead pastors in large membership churches; (2) researching leadership styles and issues of lead women pastors—the research to be both quantitative and qualitative; (3) facilitating a coaching program between current lead women pastors and other women pastors identified by bishops and cabinets as having potential to serve large churches.

To meet the first goal of the project, the LWPP leadership team planned and hosted an opening retreat for the sixty-four lead women pastors initially identified in 2004 by the General Board of Finance and Administration to launch the project (and a second retreat seven months later). We introduced the clergywomen to Blackboard, a distance learning program that we used to foster networking and discussion and to gather information. We divided the clergywomen into chat groups and conducted a series of chats during the year. The women read and discussed books on leadership.

The second goal of the LWPP was the research component. The quantitative aspect consisted of an online survey sent to the ninety-four lead women pastors (identified in 2008) and a randomly selected sample of three hundred male lead pastors of large churches.[12] The survey sought to obtain data on demographics, career trajectory, leadership styles, and issues faced by clergy. Qualitative data was also obtained from online chats, the discussion board, case studies, and interviews. A full report on the survey can be found in Appendix A. We have summarized some of the survey findings below. They revealed seven key issues for lead women pastors. For this book we invited the clergywomen to write about their own experience with and reflection on each of these issues. Due to confidentiality and the unfeasibility of obtaining permission from the congregations they serve, we do not identify which clergywoman wrote which essay, but biographies of our contributors are included at the end. We have devoted a chapter to each of these issues, which include:

Leadership Styles: This chapter relays the experience of women clergy on how their gender affects (but does not determine) how they lead and how people respond to their leadership.

Work and Family: Chapter 2 highlights how balancing work and family is a thorny challenge, and clergywomen who lead big churches share poignant stories about marriage and family. These narratives provide wisdom on how women can be senior pastors in a tall steeple church and still be attentive to family, without falling prey to the "superwoman syndrome."

Preaching and Worship: Since preaching and worship are key to effective leadership in local church ministry, this chapter examines preaching styles of lead women pastors and relates to the project findings on clergywomen's collaborative worship leadership. Includes narratives and a narrative sermon by two lead women pastors.

The Art of Conflict Management: This chapter relates how women leaders manage conflict compared with their male counterparts. Clergywomen will describe the art of dealing with conflict and share their personal stories.

Resource Management: Staffing and Finances: This chapter looks at how the lead women pastors manage staff and finances and their level of confidence in these activities. It will include wisdom from clergywomen in specific cases.

Women and the Political Process: The political process of the church assignment can be a minefield. This chapter explores how women navigate hierarchy, bureaucracy, and patriarchal systems. It also discusses how women mobilize women in a political process and identifies strategies that women use to support each other.

Women's Leadership and Spirituality: Chapter 7 explores what spirituality has to do with leadership for women and how a well-developed spiritual life is a resource for lead women pastors. It provides some of the actual spiritual practices of lead women pastors, which readers can practice in their daily lives for leadership formation.

We learned that 77 percent of lead women pastors developed their leadership style by having role models, a fact that provided validity for developing a coaching program for future lead women pastors. Some of these lead women pastors currently serving large churches are participating in coaching training and have been paired with clergywomen who have been identified as potentially serving a large church. They have covenanted to work together to understand the issues and challenges of leading a large church.

Women's Leadership and Coaching: Chapter 8 analyzes the process of coaching as a means of cultivating women's leadership for the church. It provides actual experiences of women who have been involved in a coaching relationship and how that experience has empowered their leadership. It is our hope that leaders, including those in coaching relationships, will read and study this book together.

Our Conclusion draws together insights from the data and storytelling and leads us to make recommendations to and beyond the connectional structure of the church, including seminaries and local churches, for encouraging and sustaining women's leadership. The Rev. Patricia Farris, senior pastor of First United Methodist Church in Santa Monica, California, writes an epilogue to help us think further about future possibilities and to empower the work of women in the church and society.

The following is a synopsis of the LWPP survey:

Age, Race, and Marital Status: Sixty-five percent (61) of lead women pastors (LWP) and 70 percent (139) of lead male pastors (LMP) responded to the survey. Ninety-nine percent of the survey respondents were white. We received responses from one Asian and one African American LMP and one African American lead woman pastor, clearly indicating a dearth of ethnic lead pastors in large churches. According to a 2000 *United Methodist Clergywomen Retention Study* conducted by the Anna Howard Shaw Center of Boston University, Caucasian women may find acceptance somewhat easier in local churches than racial-ethnic women.[13] (For purposes of this book, the term "racial-ethnic" is used to refer to women of any race or from any ethnic group other than white.) The LWPP study confirmed that this was true for lead women pastors.

Lead women pastors are an average of three years younger than lead male pastors, but LWP have served slightly more appointments than their male counterparts before becoming lead pastor of a large church. Sixty-nine percent of LWP are married, compared to 99 percent of LMP, a gap that is greater than for the general population. One factor that causes clergywomen to suffer, according to Barbara Zikmund, et.al. is "role strain." The role strain of clergywomen results from "role hegemony," in which stereotypes of certain gender roles provoke overt discrimination and a lack of acceptance.[14] The role strain that clergywomen experience in their ministry could partly explain the fact that one third of LWP are not married. In online chats divorced clergywomen spoke of the strains that following one's call and the activity of ministry itself put on marriage. Without speculating too much on what the data indicate, suffice it to say that it challenges the church toward consistency in inclusivity. These factors raised the issue of balancing work and family, which two clergywomen have written about in chapter 2. **Education, Career, and Salary:** More LWP were educated in the denomination-related seminaries than LMP. More LWP have doctoral degrees than LMP. More LWP are second-career clergy than LMP. More women than men have served as a district superintendent (supervisor of clergy) prior to an appointment to lead a large church. According to the survey, LWP have an average of four appointments and men an average of 3.75 appointments before becoming a lead pastor. Forty-nine percent of LWP took five appointments compared to 31 percent for LMP. More LWPs have been associate pastors in large churches prior to serving as lead pastors than have men. More LWP have been candidates for episcopacy in the past than LMP.

It was interesting to learn that seven males and one female became lead pastors in their first appointments. Does this mean that these pastors already had leadership qualities that large churches demand when first entering into ministry? Or does this mean that more of those who determine clergy appointments perceive that males have a higher capability of leading a large church?

It was also interesting to find out that one-fourth of LWP and one-third of LMP are second-career clergy who had been teachers, in business, or had military careers. Clergy who bring different skills into their ministry may do well in a large church ministry context; perhaps previous leadership and teaching skills that deal with diverse opinions and deeper understandings of finances are expected in the large church setting. The church needs to recognize and use skills that second-career clergy bring into ordained ministry, especially in the leadership of large churches.

This correlates with the most challenging issues for women in ministry today. Both LWP and LMP agree that the appointment or assignment process is one of the most challenging issues within the UMC structure. LWP tend to serve in suburbs of large cities, while more LMP serve large churches that are located in mid-size and small towns.

This study showed that more clergywomen than men earned more than $100,000. The LWP survey respondents earned slightly more than the LMP. According to the Lewis Center for Church Leadership, this finding does not match other reports about clergy salary. For example, the one hundred largest congregations of the UMC are served by male clergy (with one exception that we have been able to identify). The majority of the male respondents of this survey are serving in the middle and bottom third of the large churches.[15] A very few LWP are serving the top one-third of the largest churches, and their average salaries are about 27 percent lower than LMP. In terms of education, the Barna Research Group concurs from a random sample of Protestant churches that women in the pulpit are generally more highly educated than are their male counterparts. Currently, more than three-quarters of female pastors (77 percent) have a seminary degree. Among male pastors less than two-thirds (63 percent) can make that same claim. Despite their higher educational attainment, the study revealed, female pastors have smaller compensation levels than do male pastors.[16] The clergywomen's thoughts on these and other issues are found in chapter 6 on women and political process.

Leadership (Work Load): A significant finding in this study is that the average membership and worship attendance of churches served by LWPs are higher than the churches served by male respondents, because most of the male respondents were serving smaller-size churches than LWP respondents. The average worship attendance of churches served by LWP is higher than that of churches served by the male respondents in this study. Lead Women Pastors' churches have more weekly services on average than the congregations served by the male pastors.[17] LWPs spend more time in pastoral care than LMPs. LWPs also had more full-time staff (ten or more, an average of an additional two more staff than LMPs), and some lead pastors reported that they have to supervise more than twenty different staff positions. The data show that LWPs have more responsibilities than LMP in a similar context. Given the prominence of preaching and worship leadership for clergy, the lead women pastors share how they engage these ministries in chapter 3. A dialogue sermon preached by the Rev. Trudy Robinson and the Rev. Patricia Farris at a LWPP event is included for both the content and preaching style they represent.

Leadership Style: As much as women (and men) would like to believe that gender makes no difference (a good leader is a good leader), the reality experienced by many women clergy is that their gender affects (but does not determine) how they lead and how people respond to their leadership. Leadership style was defined as "relatively consistent patterns of interaction that typify leaders as individuals."[18] Though there were similarities between the men and women respondents on leadership style, the overwhelming majority of both the LWP and the LMP in this survey noted that they perceive gender differences in leadership, though many qualified their statements to avoid blanket generalizations. The survey revealed that men and women agree that there are different standards for clergy men and women. Men are given a standing of authority often not present for women.

Slightly more women identified their leadership style as collaborative. More LWP lead change by "informally planting seeds and hop[ing] they take root" and LMP are more likely to lead change by "intentionally recruiting support from individuals and groups." LWP are more likely to engage in collegial efforts in terms of dealing with conflicts and financial issues. LWP are less likely to openly display emotion than their male counterparts. Women reflect on their leadership styles in chapter 1. Other traits that are valued by both male and female lead pastors are strong spiritual grounding, excellence in preaching (hours spent in preparation), and strong financial leadership. The lead women pastors provided a distinctive emphasis on spiritual practices found in chapter 7.

The top two challenging issues for male and female clergy are finances and staffing. More than 60 percent of LWP reported that their confidence level with financial management has improved and their skills of managing finance have changed since becoming a LWP. More LWP use indirect communication, through other leaders in the congregation, about stewardship. More LMP feel more comfortable talking about money directly. More LWP (49 percent) reported that they feel confident in fund-raising than LMP (34 percent). However, only 33 percent of LWP reported that they feel confident in church finances, compared to 58 percent of LMP. Lead women pastors' comments on staffing and finances may be found in chapter 5 on Resource Management.

LWP reported fewer major conflicts for the last two years than LMP and more LWP considered conflict something to be avoided, according to the survey. For example, more LWP would rather ignore the situation if they are verbally attacked by a parishioner in a meeting. Staff, changes in worship style, and finances are top conflict sources among lead pastors,[19] and the lead women pastors express their experiences with these in chapter 5.

In the Blackboard discussions, chats, and interviews, the lead women pastors noted that sexism is alive and well in the church. The women noted that there is an "undercurrent" in the church that a male is needed to "handle" a large church. Here are some of the things the LWP said:

- "Women are very much still on trial in the large church. Authority is not automatically given to a woman because she is in the role of lead pastor."
- "Women have to walk a tightrope about how they dress, speak, and show emotion."

- "I was told my voice in preaching is not low enough."
- "My male associate pastor is often assumed by new people to be the senior pastor."
- "I was asked by an SPRC member if the church could have a formal arrangement with a nearby church with a male senior pastor, so that when men wanted to talk to a pastor and did not want to talk to a woman, they would have someone to go to."
- "As a part of a clergy couple, I am often introduced as the preacher's wife."
- "When men fail, they say that it was a bad fit. If a woman fails, she is more likely to feel responsible or to be blamed."
- "I find that male clergy are more likely to ask for an appointment to a large church—are more likely to voice their needs to a Cabinet."
- "For a bishop to be a woman is more acceptable, 'easier to take' than a woman as pastor of a large church."
- "Women tend to say, 'Send me where I'm needed.' Women are conditioned to wait to be asked (for a date, asked to dance, etc.). We need to up our confidence level about self-identifying to serve the large church."

We learned that lead women pastors still serve large churches as pioneers. Ninety percent of women said that they were the first woman pastor serving as a lead pastor in their current appointment. Seventy-five percent of lead women pastors believe that serving a large church is a special call. Their understanding that they've been called by God to serve this particular setting sustains their strength and integrity. Their leadership styles appear generally more collaborative, relational, equipping, diplomatic, discreet, equipping, directive, prophetic, delegatory, confident, decisive, creative, adaptive, compassionate, and less confrontational in conflict than lead men pastors in this study. Even though there is still evidence of a glass ceiling (only one ethnic LWP, only one woman serving the top one hundred of the largest United Methodist churches), some cracks have definitely been made! Since 2008 when the project began, the number of lead women pastors in The United Methodist Church has increased from sixty-four to one hundred and thirty-seven as of January, 2013. The experiences of these lead women pastors will serve as a resource for the formation of younger generations of women leadership for not only the UMC but also in our society. Bring on the lead women pastors!

Notes

1. According to the Association of Theological Schools (ATS), 445 more female students were enrolled in theological schools than male students in 2011. Table 2.14-B: Head Count Enrollment by Degree Programs, Age, and Gender, Fall 2011, United States.
2. http://www.youtube.com/watch?v=8-ci63EYAzc.
3. Kathe Schaaf, et al., eds. *Women, Spirituality and Transformative Leadership: Where Grace Meets Power* (Woodstock, VT: Skylight Paths Publishing, 2012), 4.
4. Dana Milbank, "A Thank-You for 18 Million Cracks in the Glass Ceiling," *Washington Post,* June 8, 2008.
5. Barbara Kellerman and Deborah L. Rhode, eds. *Women and Leadership: The State of Play and Strategies for Change* (San Francisco: Jossey-Bass, 2007), 1, 6.
6. Ibid., 16. Two examples of said research are "The Bottom Line: Connecting Corporate Performance and Gender Diversity" (research report), Catalyst Knowledge Center website, January 15, 2004, http://www.catalyst.org/knowledge/bottom-line-connecting-corporate-performance-and-gender-diversity; and "The Special Report: Women in Business," *Economist*, July 23, 2005, 64.
7. Such as the Clergywomen's Retention Study of the Anna Howard Shaw Center, Boston University School of Theology, October 1997. A second study was begun in 2010.
8. Salaries for United Methodist Clergy in the U.S. Context. The General Board of Higher Education and Ministry of The United Methodist Church, 2010. http://www.gbhem.org/atf/cf/%7B0bcef929-bdba-4aa0-968f-d1986a8eef80%7D/DOM_SalaryStudyPacket.pdf.
9. http://www.barna.org/barna-update/article/17-leadership/304-number-of-female-senior-pastors-in-protestant-churches.
10. The 2006 consultation was sponsored by the clergy lifelong learning office of The General Board of Higher Education and Ministry (GBHEM). The 1956 general conference passed

legislation approving the ordination of women. The United Brethren Church had ordained women since the 1880s, but their merger with the Evangelical Church complicated matters. However, some women continued to be ordained in the Evangelical United Brethren church, which merged with the Methodist Church in 1968. See Mark Chaves, *Ordaining Women: Culture and Conflict in Religious Organizations* (Cambridge: Harvard University Press, 1997), 23.

11. A lead pastor of a large membership church was defined by the General Council of Finance and Administration as clergy who are serving churches with one thousand or more members within the UMC. As of December 31, 2004, there were 34,659 UM churches in the U.S. Of those, 1,154 had a membership of one thousand or greater, and 64 of those churches had a woman as lead pastor. In October 2008, the office of clergy lifelong learning at GBHEM identified 94 lead women pastors of large churches. Note the increase in lead women pastors since 2004. We recognize the arbitrariness of the one-thousand figure and the fluctuating membership rolls of local congregations, and that some locales and denominations will differ in what constitutes a big church.

12. The survey was prepared by the LWPP leadership team, and statistical analysis was provided by the Lewis Center for Church Leadership of Wesley Theological Seminary. www.churchleadership.com.

13. *The United Methodist Clergywomen Retention Study* (Anna Howard Shaw Center: Boston University School of Theology, 2000), http://www.bu.edu/sth/shaw/retention/chapter-two.html.

14. Barbara Brown Zikmund, Adair T. Lummis, and Patricia M.Y. Chang. *Clergy Women: An Uphill Calling* (Louisville, KY: Westminster John Knox Press, 1998), 23, 189.

15. Based on 2007 report, large churches have three levels in The UMC: the small size (1,000-1,272 members), the medium size (1,273–1,809 members), and the large size (1,810 or more members). Among the small-size churches women and men who serve make comparable salaries: women are paid about 2 per-

cent more. Among the medium-size large churches, men are paid about 4 percent more. Among the large-size large churches men receive 27 percent more than women. Lovett H. Weems Jr., Ann A. Michel, Joseph E. Arnold, and Tana Brown, *Report on Lead Pastor Survey Conducted by The General Board of Higher Education and Ministry,* Fall 2008, 2.

16. http://www.barna.org/barna-update/article/17-leadership/304-number-of-female-senior-pastors-in-protestant-churches.

17. Thirty-two percent of LWP have four weekly services compared to 16 percent of LMP.

18. Alice H. Eagly and Linda L. Carli, *Through the Labyrinth: The Truth About How Women Become Leaders* (Center for Public Leadership) (Cambridge: Harvard Business School Press, 2007), 133.

19. Twenty-three percent of LWP reported that there have been major conflicts over the past two years compared to 37 percent of LMP. Two percent of LWP experienced conflicts related to sexual misconduct over the past two years, compared to 8 percent of LMP.

CHAPTER 1
LEADERSHIP STYLES

Editor's Note
The data from the LWPP revealed similarities between the men and women's leadership styles; however, the overwhelming majority of both female and male clergy in our survey noted that they perceive gender differences in leadership. More women identified their leadership style as collaborative and said they lead change by planting seeds and building consensus. Lead women pastors are less likely to openly display emotion than their male counterparts, notwithstanding the stereotype of women being more emotional than men. Our research revealed that men and women agree that there are different standards for clergy men and women. Men are given a standing of authority often not present for women. Cultural identity also adds another layer to the variety of styles. Here is what two clergywomen wrote about their leadership styles.

Spirit-Led Leadership
It took me many months to say yes to my current appointment to a large church. Over the past forty years, this church grew from just a handful of members to many thousands. It is recognized within the city, as well as across the nation, as a leading institution for progressive causes. This has much to do with the leadership of my predecessor. A charismatic, iconic leader, his bold vision is legendary. Even though he is officially retired, he is still actively engaged in the leadership of the church.

In my many months of discernment, I questioned whether I had the spiritual resources, the necessary skills, and the ego strength to pastor under such unusual circumstances. I spent time in prayer as well as study, researching the history of large church transitions, particularly those that have transferred from a strong, charismatic leader. Sadly, I discovered that there is very little research in this area! I finally said yes, feeling that both my academic background and ministry experience would assist a community that, with the eventual passing of this strong leader, would need a lot of expertise and care.

Each day, as I make my way to my office, I say a very short prayer: *Dear God, please help me check my ego at the door.* This prayer has resulted in an unanticipated consequence. It has freed me in ways I hadn't anticipated. I realized that my ego has been very invested in my ministry in the past. It was my ego that caused me to work long hours at the expense of my mental and physical health. It was my ego that caused me to refer to "my" church, "my" parishioners, and "my" vision. It was my ego that caused a blurring of boundaries around where my ministry ended and my parishioners' began. Often, I would default to "I can do it better and more efficiently," blocking the spiritual and leadership growth of congregational members. As I prepared to serve this large church, which still was very captivated by the strong, charismatic leadership of my predecessor, I recognized that there was no room for my ego in this space, and, in fact, my ego would take a severe beating if I did try to bring it here! I began to break free of this ego orientation and to ground myself in a more spiritual alignment. The result? *I have moved from being ego-driven to being Spirit-led.*

As I have learned to be Spirit-led, discernment has taken a center role in my decision-making, congregational development, and leadership empowerment. It's no longer all about me, but instead it is about how God is moving in this community, what opportunities for faithful discipleship God is offering, and who God is lifting up as new leaders. My job is to listen, plan, implement, and empower.

Being Spirit-led has allowed me to think out of the box and respond creatively to ministry opportunities. There is no road map based on the success stories of my colleagues, no tool box that others have used that I must fall back on. Instead, I am able to reflect on my unique social location and ministry milieu and allow the

Spirit to raise up programs and possibilities that are indigenous to the people I serve.

By not being ego-driven, I can present ministry ideas without feeling that they must succeed at any and all cost. My own sense of self-worth is no longer based on "succeeding." If something is in sync with the Spirit's desires, it will move forward. This frees me to be open to and even welcome failure, which then leads to greater insight and growth. When a program does flourish, we all get to celebrate, because I do not feel the need to own it as "mine." This empowers the community to take greater ownership of the ministry we share and to add their dreams for new ministry opportunities. My job as a spiritual leader is to help them foster spiritual practices that will keep them in tune with the Spirit's leading, to help them recognize where God is showing up, so that they will dare to step boldly into the risks and possibilities of faithful discipleship.

ACTS of a Steel Magnolia

I often ask myself, "Who am I?" It's not because I am lost, but because I don't want to get lost. Since I have driven off the track of traditional thought and was tossed out of fixed boxes a long time ago, I have to find my own stream as I swim through life. I am a 1.5 generation (bilingual/ bi-cultural, born and raised to age eighteen in Korea) Korean American clergywoman who has been serving in cross-racial and cross-cultural appointments for almost two decades in The United Methodist Church. Additionally, I am single, five feet tall with a sharp tongue, and a former Presbyterian. If I were standing on a baseball field, I'd have three strikes against me and would be out of the game. Interestingly, in spite of all these strikes (some might call them handicaps), I am still here and I am grateful that I am standing in God's mission field. It has been my responsibility to make these strikes become home runs. I believe that is the beauty of God's intention in my life. Consequently, I need to work three times harder to handle the attacks of foul balls such as racism, sexism, or classism that pop up.

If I see my image positively, I can enjoy life freely and go back and forth happily between these two cultures. However, the flip side of the coin tells me that I am not fully accepted in either place. This tension demands that I exert an extra effort to be accepted. I have to put all my being into each stroke to swim against the current or to hurtle over intervening dams. It is not easy. In fact, it is hard work, but I never intend to give up.

Although Korean American churches have come a long way to be open and inclusive, they still do not fully acknowledge a clergy-woman's authority or welcome a woman as their pastor. Even though I am bilingual and bicultural, I was not particularly interested in serving Korean American churches, but felt distinctly called to serve cross-racial and cross-cultural churches. I wanted to experience, embrace, and contribute to a genuinely inclusive, worldwide, global church. However, like Korean American churches, Anglo churches initially do not open their arms and welcome an ethnic Asian woman as their leader. People are curious about me, but doubtful and cautious. It usually takes time to prove my leadership ability and skills. I am not afraid of challenges because I think my call is to tackle them.

Interestingly, in general, people still have stereotypical images of Asian women: exotic, mysterious, quiet, and submissive. For my congregants, however, it doesn't take long to change their previous misconceptions. I don't talk much, but articulate my thoughts clearly and speak my mind frankly, assertively, and straightforwardly. I smile often, but act fast and forcefully. Basically, I am an open book—they get what they see. They learn to like my transparency, openness, and flexibility. Actually, I assume that they don't know what to do with this "small woman with a thundering voice," and my nicknames include "steel magnolia," "tough cookie," and "smiling bulldog."

Whenever I move to a new church, I express my mind to the congregation: "If there are areas that you find lacking in my ministry (such as preaching, administration, pastoral care), I'll be more than willing to work harder to improve myself. However, if you have any problems with my ethnicity, gender, and size, you have to deal with God directly because God created me as I am."

An example of this directness happened about fifteen years ago, at my second appointed church. A middle-aged man tried to push my buttons with his arrogant, condescending attitude. He looked like Moses—tall, big, heavy, vigorous, with a white beard and a cool look in his leather jacket. He tried to project himself as stern. One day, he and I were involved in a tense dialogue.

At one point, I looked up and said, "Don, you are tall, big, strong, and tough; I am short, small, and fragile looking. But, do you know what? I am very fast and quick. I can turn around and kick your butt anytime. Behave yourself!" I still remember the shocked look on Don's face—his deep blue eyes were about to pop out, his jaw dropped, and he lost his words. That was a defining moment for me. That was the moment when all my fear, anger, and frustration of men (especially white men) drifted away and I felt freed. I had never lost my ground when I debated with any man, but somehow I felt this time as though I hit the right spot. Of course, I don't use this straightforward method (shock treatment) every time: I use my gift of discernment to handle the situation of ill behaving people. Don turned into a genial lamb and became an ardent supporter in my ministry.

Gathering many other experiences, I've come up with my own leadership motto. I believe leadership is not the words used, but the actions taken. Since I like to play with words, I keep ideas in mind by using acronyms. My leadership motto is ACTS: A for Attitude, C for Communication, T for Training, and S for Service.

Attitude: My attitude toward relationships, projects, or vision determines its success. It is not only my potential, ability, and skills, but my positive attitude with an upbeat personality, inner resiliency/tenacity, and gumption that motivate and lead. Attitude energizes and helps me keep a spirit of excellence in whatever I do. As a leader, many important decisions are strengthened by my attitude. Therefore, I need to be the cheerleader for myself and others.

Communication: I am not talking about technical communication skills, but the ability to lead a conversation with listening ears and confident speaking skills. To be effective, I study human behaviors and practice speech exercises. Both verbal and nonverbal languages are important mediums to connect people heart to heart. In my own interpretation, communication means "come-unification," and the main purpose of it is to come together in unity through clarification/clarity. By being open, flexible, and non-judgmental, I try to reach out to others horizontally.

Training: The most important task for a pastor is to equip congregants to be disciples of Jesus Christ. For that goal, I need to train them through preaching, teaching, and healing/caring, but I have to discipline myself first. I try to keep up a life of daily prayers, reflections and meditation, regular fasting and retreats. Leadership requires maintaining a balance between spiritual, emotional, and physical dimensions. I try to train myself to be a resource person to empower others.

Service: Leadership is not just what people say or how they talk, but a "walk the talk" exercise. Setting a good example of servant leadership is my ultimate lifestyle. I believe that people learn from seeing and imitating a good role model. No more words are needed. ACTS lead.

In order to serve the body of Christ, I yoke my Eastern (Korean) and Western (American) backgrounds, heritage, and cultures. The struggle and tension is the "geeing and hawing" of these two enormous influences on my life. Geeing and hawing refers to the tugging and pulling of two horses or oxen yoked together. The farmer calls out for the team to gee (go right) or haw (go left); if one gees and the other haws they are not working as a team—all work stops, nothing gets done. This farming term is a nice analogy of the inner struggle of one who yokes her Eastern and Western cultures together.

It is a privilege to experience the benefits and advantages of these two currents and to swim in and out to create my own little eddy for God. For example, in my formative church and family, members practiced early morning devotions and gave generous tithes and thanksgiving offerings to the church. Now, I offer daily early morning services during Lent, and ask my congregants to join me. After Lent, I continue to offer a weekly midweek morning prayer service. Prayer life is the center of my parish and many adopt it well.

Also, I express my caring and gratitude through gourmet food. I enjoy cooking and love to spread a feast. At seminary, I invited so many people to my dinners that I earned the title "the Founder of Banquet Theology" at seminary. I applied this experience to my ministry. It helped establish the ministries of hospitality, generosity, and thanksgiving. When I visit people at their homes, I take flowers from the altar or something I cooked. I have served countless dumplings, Korean barbecue, chicken soup, sausage and peppers, and items from international menus. Each year, I invite the church leaders to a dinner that I prepare and invite the whole congregation to the pastor's love feast (luncheon) after a Sunday service.

I try to be a leader who keeps the balance of "yin" and "yang" in my style and ministry—cool but warm, stern but flexible, sharp but gentle, direct but compassionate, intelligent but humble, tough but understanding. Whatever struggles we experience in the church, I treat as growing pains for all of us to activate the vision for the kingdom of God. I sincerely believe that, with love in my heart, God will provide leadership not only of wisdom, patience, energy, and passion, but will also melt the walls of fear of change that create the prejudices of racism, sexism, and classism. For these ACTS we pray, all to the glory of God.

Questions for Reflection
1. Kathe Schaaf, Kay Lindahl, and others in *Women, Spirituality and Transformative Leadership* claim that women with unique gifts and ways of knowing are being called forth at this time in history for service in a world that needs their particular contribution. They quote Meg Wheatley's definition of leadership, "A leader is anyone who is willing to help." So women have been leaders in their families and communities throughout history. Though their leadership skills have seldom been recognized, these are precisely, Schaaf and Lindahl say, the skills that are needed in the world (and the church, we might add) today. What do you think about this definition and this claim?
2. When you have exercised either Spirit-led or ego-driven leadership, what were the results?

3. Share about your own leadership style and how you came to develop it.
4. How do you think your gender and culture or even size influence or impact your leadership?
5. The second clergywoman in this chapter was called a "steel magnolia" or a "smiling bulldog." What would be a good nickname for your leadership style? What are the ACTS of your leadership style?

Editor's Note

Clergywomen identified the balancing of ministry and family responsibilities as one of their top two most challenging issues. More lead women pastors named this issue than male pastors in our survey. Though society is gradually changing with men picking up more responsibility for the family and home, women still bear most of the caregiving roles; for some this is by conscious or unconscious choice. Two clergywomen share how they navigated this in their situations.

Support in Difficult Circumstances

My husband and I met at Duke Divinity School in 1976. We married soon after, fully expecting to serve as pastors in our respective denominations of United Methodism and United Church of Christ for the rest of our lives. But in 1991, about two years after the birth of our second child, my husband began exhibiting strange symptoms. He developed a head palsy and began falling. After several doctor visits, he was diagnosed with cerebellar ataxia, a debilitating and progressive neuromuscular disorder similar to Lou Gehrig's and Parkinson diseases, but not as well known, nor with any known treatment.

The diagnosis was brutal: within five years he would be confined to a wheelchair and in ten years totally bedridden. Needless to say, we were devastated. We had two small children, were both pastors of small churches, and my husband was working on a PhD at Florida State University. This was not how we planned to spend our lives. We both went into a tailspin, but my partner in life completely shut down on me. We had never planned on living off one income; in fact the two incomes we had were not enough to really cover our needs, and because my spouse became depressed, he quit his PhD program and stopped working at the church. We struggled financially, physically, mentally, and emotionally. I began frantically trying to find a way to sustain my spiritual and emotional life, as well as be there for my hurting spouse and our two girls, all the while being pastor of a small town church.

For the next twenty-some years I felt I had three full-time jobs: mother to our two girls, pastor of churches, and nurse/comforter/friend to my husband. The later reality was not as brutal as first diagnosed—he just went into a wheelchair full-time about 2007 and is able to get around with some help—but the disease took its toll on all of us. He continued to have many periods of depression, his physical condition deteriorated, and our girls grew up basically watching me be both parents. However, we got through it.

I have served four churches since his diagnosis, with each church being larger and more demanding. I learned to work with staff, church administration, building committees, and all the demands of running a church, and balance my life at home, raising our girls and helping my husband deal with his disease both physically and emotionally. But I didn't do this alone. With each move, I made myself establish boundaries. I knew that I needed to get away for times with fellow clergy, especially women, and participate in continuing education events.

But the most important thing I did was join support groups. At all my churches, I joined at least two clergy support groups. These included one-on-one relationships of women clergy with weekly lunches and meetings, and intentional leadership support group meetings with clergy. In these support groups, we share about personal life issues and challenges in ministry, and read leadership books and examine case studies. I found I could do what I needed in the church and at home because I had people I could go to for support and encouragement. I also developed an intentional devotional time, found time for daily prayer walks, took care of my own health, and regularly took my days off and four weeks of vacation.

I am in my last few years of ministry. I have decided to retire after reaching forty years of ministry. (I probably would have gone to age seventy if I didn't know that my husband would continue to get worse.) But I am at peace with my decision and continue to marvel at the wonderful ministry and life I have had. Our girls have grown into wonderful young women and are kind, loving, caring, and joyful people with great lives of their own. They continue to provide support and love to both of us. My present church is very loving and giving and I am really enjoying my ministry with it. This is a challenging church and area as it is very diverse with many economic problems. But the church is healthy. I have a large staff and continue to marvel at how we work together.

As I look back over my ministry, I find I did the best I could do. But again, I did this with help. The most important thing I did with all my struggles was to find support. I did this willingly and intentionally and am glad I did.

You Can Have It All . . . It Takes Discipline

As one who was called to ministry at the age of thirteen, I spent considerable time observing how the people in my life balanced their career and family. In particular, I watched how pastors (most of whom men) faced the challenge of pastoring a church and spending quality time with family. My childhood upbringing and home life was a product of this age-old challenge.

My late father was a United Methodist pastor, and I spent most of my childhood in a parsonage. My father was a well-respected pastor in the church and in the community, and yet we who were closest to him felt like we knew him least. Although family was a priority for my dad, he had a difficult time managing to spend quality time with the family. My mother, a school teacher, would often have to play a dual parenting role to keep harmony in the home.

When I said yes to God, my greatest concern was whether I would have to choose between being a pastor and raising a family. I had a strong sense of call to be a wife and mother, but I had also witnessed firsthand the complexity of ministry and all of its demands. By the grace of God, today I celebrate twenty years in ministry, and I am celebrating nineteen years of marriage and am a mother to two daughters, fourteen and ten years old.

For many years women were told, "You can't have it all. You have to make a choice between raising a family or having a career." I have learned that you can have it all . . . but it takes discipline. Over the course of these twenty years I have served inner-city and suburban churches both large and small.

Prior to serving as a district superintendent, I served as senior pastor of a large downtown church. It had a membership of one thousand members and its weekly services averaged about six hundred worshippers. It was a multi-staffed church with many and varied services, small groups, missions, and outreach ministries. The ministry and staff demanded so much of my attention and involvement on many levels. I found it helpful that I learned very early in my ministry career that I needed to set clear boundaries around my time and availability. This learning served me well in this ministry setting. I have regularly reminded myself that if family was my priority, then I had to be intentional about making time for them.

One of the boundaries I set in my ministry was directly related to scheduling. I made it known that I would not schedule myself regularly to be at the church more than three nights a week and no more than two nights consecutively. This included not only church meetings but Bible studies, small groups, etc. I also committed to ending meetings no later than 8:30 pm. Although this was a new concept for many, and a radical change for others, my boundary-setting led us into a much needed broader conversation about stewardship of time, balance of work and family, busyness, and ministry burnout among laity and church staff. I realized over time that members' expectations for clergy leadership can be greatly shaped and re-shaped by how the clergy communicates his or her vision and expectations regarding leadership and priorities.

Here are some practical suggestions that will help you balance work and family:
• Discipline yourself to allow personal and family time in the midst

of your busy work schedule.

- Set realistic goals and expectations for your work and commitments.
- Schedule quality time with your family.
- Align your calendar with your priorities.
- Take time for personal sabbath.
- Clearly communicate your priorities to your church leaders, staff, and membership.
- Serve as a healthy model for balancing family and work for your members and staff.
- Refrain from being a workaholic . . . you have been called and appointed and don't need to prove yourself. Make a choice to live a balanced life.

Questions for Reflection

1. When have you experienced "role strain" (see the Introduction)? What personal difficulties and/or sacrifices have you made? What resources do you have for difficult personal circumstances? How might you cultivate those resources? What keeps you keeping on?
2. Describe when you may have felt the pressure to be a superwoman.
3. Some more conservative groups have postulated that family and home have suffered in society since women moved into leadership roles. What would be your answer to this sentiment?
4. How do you negotiate the responsibilities for family and home with your spouse or others?
5. How do you feel about "having it all"? What is your discipline or "rule of life" for keeping balance?
6. Do you think that some gifted and called women may "hold back" from leadership because of family responsibilities? What is your own view of the balance? What would you say to those women?

CHAPTER 3
PREACHING AND WORSHIP

Editor's Note

Preaching and worship leadership were named by the clergywomen as being two of their most prominent gifts. In online chats the lead women pastors expressed that being a good preacher is one of the most important (if not the most important) qualities of leadership for a pastor of a large church. A significant finding of our study was that worship attendance is slightly higher in the churches served by the lead women pastors than those served by men. Clergywomen spend more hours in sermon preparation and tend to be collaborative in how they plan worship. Here are stories of how two women lead pastors approach worship leadership. We have included a sermon preached by Patricia Farris and Trudy Robinson at one of the LWP events, demonstrating their collaborative style.

The Joys of Collaborative Worship with God's People

"Praise the Lord! How good it is to sing praises to our God; for [God] is gracious, and a song of praise is fitting." (Psalm 147:1)

Early in my ministry I resolved to make the Scripture text for each Sunday the centerpiece of worship, so that every element of our worship would speak to the text if at all possible. What I had come to realize is that people experience God's Word on many levels, not just through the preached word of the sermon. My question for each week was, "How can we bring the text alive for our people?"

It also became clear to me that worship planning was too important to be done alone. Liturgy is the work of the people. But in my first appointment I had no staff and very few volunteers, so I met monthly with other clergywomen to gain from their support and creativity. We would each bring something for the Scripture texts for the months to come. Sometimes it was an exegesis of a particular text, a well-crafted prayer, a meaningful illustration, or simply a list of questions derived from the text. We would then take the gifts we had each brought and go home inspired anew to write our sermons and design our worship experiences.

Since those early days of preaching, now more than twenty-eight years ago, I have benefitted from the joy of planning, designing, and leading worship that came about not merely from my prayerful work with God's Holy Spirit, but through the collaborative efforts of a worship team I learned to gather. Just as the variety of gifts blessed us all in those gatherings of clergywomen, I have found the same richness working with my musicians, altar guild members, worship committees, and dedicated volunteers.

I was the senior pastor of a large church that had both traditional and contemporary worship styles. In our contemporary service we regularly used PowerPoint with the sermons, video clips from movies and skits, live drama, and altar and stage settings that spoke to the Scripture text and its theme for the day. While I often was still preaching from the lectionary, I had learned that people are drawn to themes and images. I found that our people responded well to sermon series. I made it my spiritual discipline to plan my sermon texts and resulting series at least six months ahead. I would share those texts on a spreadsheet with my worship team and list possible themes and images I wanted to use. I would ask them to pray over the texts and come prepared to our quarterly planning sessions with their own ideas and insights about the texts. At that planning meeting we would bring our collective thoughts together and solidify our directions. We each left with assignments.

My associate pastor and youth pastor researched movie clips and skits. My associate pastor and I shared preaching responsibilities; when one of us preached the other did the prayers. We were careful to craft our pastoral prayers along the themes of the day. My young adult volunteer who was a graphic designer committed to designing my weekly PowerPoint images and theme logos for advertising. Our worship chairperson took over the altar designing, and other volunteers took on the contemporary worship stage setting. The church staff met weekly, so we were in touch with one another right up to Sunday mornings about how it was all going to come together.

We were intentional about including our children and youth in our worship leadership. Although they participated through choirs, we wanted more. For example on Boy and Girl Scout Sundays we invited the scouts to help us write the liturgies for their service and then help us lead the service by reading and sometimes participating in dramas or presentations. Confirmation classes did the same. It was very common to have the Scripture texts presented as dramatic readings with people acting out the text while it was being read. Those occasions became teaching moments as we worked with the participants to explain why we did what we did in worship. We learned that when people get to be a part of planning and leading worship, it becomes more meaningful to them and they remember it for years to come.

This collaborative approach transformed how our worship team saw its role. Previously it had done its work with a focus on their specific function, with the communion stewards focusing on obtaining the communion elements and setting them up on communion Sundays and clearing them away after the services. The acolyte volunteers annually trained the new acolytes. The altar guild changed the paraments for each liturgical season, prepared for special seasons of Advent, Christmas, and Easter, and saw that the worship spaces were regularly cleaned. They had not been asked to come together and see their various worship ministries as essential parts of a holistic experience of worship. They had not been asked to pray about the Scriptures and how those Scriptures might inform how they did their various worship ministries.

With this collaborative approach the members of the worship team were encouraged to bring creativity to their tasks. The worship team chairperson enthusiastically joined with me in designing new altar and stage settings. Creative people in the congregation were invited to contribute their efforts in making new props for these settings. Even with no paid staff in a rural church, a pastor and local church volunteers can do collaborative, creative worship planning using this kind of model.

We established a communications team who worked with our worship team to publicize the upcoming worship experiences. Using the themes and logos of our worship, the communications team crafted postcards, signs, e-mails, advertisements, and business cards to let the community know what we were going to be offering. We encouraged our congregation to use the business cards as invitations to their friends and associates to attend our worship services. Worship and communications then worked with our evangelism/hospitality teams to have the congregation prepared to receive guests through excellent hospitality and intentional follow-up.

We targeted our invitational outreach to the community the weeks leading up to going back to school, inviting students and their parents to attend our worship services and participate in a "blessing of the backpacks" ceremony. We celebrated "children's sabbath" and invited the students and parents in our preschool and after-school programs. On Christmas Eve we gave out postcards illustrating our January sermon series and inviting them to worship with us in the New Year. At Easter and at our graduation Sunday we gave out postcards inviting children and youth to participate in vacation Bible school and our summer camps. We consistently tied our evangelistic outreach to our worship opportunities.

Having greatly reaped the benefits of such collaborative worship planning and leadership, it seems unthinkable to go back to planning in isolation. It also would not be a biblical model. We experienced this approach as a fulfilling of the text from Ephesians: "But speaking the truth in love, we must grow up in every way into him who is the head, into Christ, from whom the whole body, joined and knitted together by every ligament with which it is equipped, as each part is working properly, promotes the body's growth in building itself up in love" (Ephesians 4:15–16).

Those Sundays Just Keep Comin'

It's hard for me to believe, but I have preached through the lectionary about eight times now. Funny how those Sundays just keep coming. Although I offer several non-lectionary-based series each year, and although my love for Scripture is as alive as it has ever been, I was getting a little bored with my own preaching—and probably a little bit lazy in preparation. I had always preached from an outline, only writing a manuscript when it was required for a class or a publication. And for the most part, I stood behind a pulpit. I had long ago lost the mild "butterflies" that so often go along with a good sermon. I do not think my preaching was bad, but I knew it could be better.

Over a period of time, God began to encourage me to make some changes in my preaching. I no longer use a pulpit unless I want to for some particular reason, and I no longer rely on any sermon notes at all except for the Bible and the occasional quotation that I want to quote with precision. This has been, without a doubt, the biggest change in my ministry in twenty-five years. I am now mildly nervous and excited when I stand to preach, and the Lord is blessing these efforts abundantly. I am pleased to share my new homiletical methodology, for it has been a great blessing to me. Perhaps parts of it can benefit others as well.

The core of my preaching now rests in my study retreats, which are probably the most important element involved in staying on top of those Sundays that arrive so rapidly. Twice a year I make a journey to the renewal center, where I work intently for five days. I am blessed that my family and my congregation understand how important this time is for me. I bring with me several study Bibles, the lectionary, my calendar, my journal, devotional material, my walking shoes, and any additional materials that I have collected expressly for this time apart. I return home with a completed schedule detailing six months' worth of preaching, including the titles and foci of any series I might offer, and a designated text, thesis statement, and title for each preaching occasion during that six month period of time. I place the associate pastors on the preaching schedule as well, and include any mission speakers we may be hosting. A copy of this schedule is distributed to all ministry staff, the music director, and my administrative assistant. I also have collected about half an hour's worth of brainstorming material in a computer file for each of these preaching occasions. Sometimes this includes illustrative material that comes to mind, but I always seek to get a fresh perspective on the biblical text and record enough information to ensure I can recall my ideas when I look at that file months later. I have found the study retreats to be greatly beneficial for me. I am better able to relax and focus on the other tasks of ministry because I know I have a good head start on preaching for any given Sunday.

Now I'll describe what a week of sermon preparation looks like for me at this point in my ministry. On Monday I open the file for the next Sunday and review what I previously prepared with exegesis. Ideas spark more ideas, and I type in as much as I can, trying not to edit for quality at this stage. I can usually feel my energy level shift at some point, which is my indicator to stop adding new material and to begin filling out what I already have. At the end of Monday I try to have my ideas condensed and organized into a rough outline, more or less in the order in which the material will be presented. Tuesday I open the file again and begin to write a manuscript from the previous day's outline. As I work, I divide my writing into between fifteen and twenty-two paragraphs (or "sections"), which I then number. These individual sections are important for my learning process as the week continues, and I strive to make each paragraph relative to the thesis, but still brief enough that I will be able to learn its material as easily as possible. At the end of Tuesday I have a manuscript of between 1,500 and 2,500 words, depending upon how much time I have to preach in a given service of worship. For me, this represents approximately fifteen to twenty-five minutes of preaching. I have found the word count to be especially helpful, as I do not have an innate sense of how long something will take when it is just in my head.

Wednesday is the day when I prepare the PowerPoint slides to accompany the sermon, inserting numbered slide "cues" within the manuscript for the audiovisual technician running the slides on the upcoming Sunday. At the end of the day, I have e-mailed my PowerPoint presentation and the "cued" copy of my manuscript to our media center folks. I have also made a digital audio recording of the sermon, which will be used later in the week as I am learning the material for preaching.

On Thursday, it is time for me to begin learning the sermon for presentation. This is a process of memorization, but not strictly so. I am more interested in learning the key idea in each section and committing it for easy mental recall. I have tried several different methods. Since I am a visual learner, I have the most success using a visual aid to assist me in learning each discrete section. There are numerous ways to visually "block" the sections, but in my case I have fifteen to twenty-two "pictures" that I have developed based on a memory aid taught in the Dale Carnegie Course. For example, the memory "peg" for picture #1 is "1-Run," so my computer-generated picture #1 depicts a stick figure running. I then take a pen and fill in the "picture" to reflect the key points in section one. The memory peg for #2 is "2-Zoo," so my picture always includes a large zoo cage. With my pen, I fill in material that will help me visually recall the content of my second section. I continue until I have completed all fifteen to twenty-two pictures, which become my visual aids. The very act of *making* these pictures helps me learn the material, so by Thursday evening I am in good shape for the weekend.

Friday is my day off, but I allow about an hour to review my visual aids. I have found that working with the pictures randomly allows me to learn them more solidly. Typically, I use a phone app to generate my fifteen to twenty-two "numbers" in random order, and then I try to recall the content of each section as it relates to its number. By the end of the day, I have a much more solid grasp of the content of each section as a discrete entity.

Saturday is my day to spend with family, but once again I spend some time putting all of my sections together. This is where my audio recording comes in handy—I listen to the sermon, empowering my mind to envision each individual picture associated with its respective section. On a given Saturday, I listen to the entire sermon between two and five times, depending on what I am doing that day. Often I will listen to it in the car, while I work out, and at other times when I have a chance to fit it in. By bedtime I have the sense that the material will "preach" the next morning.

Early Sunday morning I get up, drink coffee, and pray. I am usually as silent as possible on Sunday mornings before the early service, but I plug my earphones into my digital recorder and listen to the sermon one time through. Then, as I drive to church later that morning, I listen to the sermon one final time during my commute. When I step up to preach, I am able to deliver the material with virtually no notes while maintaining that important eye contact with the congregation. God is faithful in empowering me to do this with passion and enthusiasm, even though I have been over the material so many times. I always feel just a little nervous, but know that once I get rolling my memory will be up to the task of remembering my sections.

After the last worship service on Sunday I really can relax, because I know I have a good start on the next week's sermon already. I seem to be able to easily "erase" the mental images from my mind, so I am starting with a blank mental canvas the next day. It is true that those Sundays just keep coming—but they are now much more joyful than they used to be!

A Dialogue Sermon by the Rev. Patricia Farris and the Rev. Trudy Robinson
(In memory of the Rev. Kathleen Baskin-Ball)

A Note from Patricia and Trudy:
We were asked to offer a dialogue sermon for the opening worship service of the Lead Women Pastors Project's closing retreat: "Of Wonder and Wisdom: A Service of Remembrance for the Rev. Kathleen Baskin-Ball." Kathleen was one of our dear lead women pastor colleagues who had died the previous year. We had all been inspired by her life and faith and saddened by her death.

Rev. Trudy had done collaborative sermons before with colleagues serving the same church, but had always been able to walk down the hallway and meet face-to-face to prepare. But this time, Rev. Patricia was in California, and Rev. Trudy was in Wyoming. While the process for and outcome of our collaboration was a bit different, the spirit of a dialogue sermon was the same. We both wanted to provide space for the other's voice to be heard, the other's insights to be offered, the other's faith to be witnessed. In the process of forming our message, we were committed to honoring our dialogue partner. We had fun learning more about each other as we listened to each other. We hope that not only our words meant something to those who heard, but the fact that we spoke together also meant something. It is not just the words we say, but the way we say them that matters.

One more caveat. Preaching is an art of communication. It is more an audio art than a visual art. Reading a sermon isn't the same thing as hearing one because the preacher is always listening to the congregation even as she speaks. When reading a sermon, the most we can hope for is for you to imagine being there, surrounded by women, eager to be together to learn from each other, to be tended by each other, to nurture, support, inspire, and heal each other through the grace of God.

"Who Are We as Daughters of Creation, Wisdom, and the Resurrection?"
Scripture readings: Psalm 104, Proverbs 3:13–18, and Matthew 28:1–10

Spoken by Patricia:
Last Sunday, as part of our Earth Day celebration, our congregation sang "I Sing the Almighty Power of God." "I sing the *wisdom* that ordained the sun to rule the day; the moon shines full at God's command and all the stars obey. While all that borrows life from thee is ever in thy care, and everywhere that we can be, thou, God, art present there." That's the theme of our worship today as we come in wonder and awe at the bountifulness of God's love and grace to weave our stories and sing God's praises. With our sister Kathleen, we are daughters of creation. We are daughters of

wisdom. We are daughters of resurrection and sisters of Mary Magdalene. Creation, wisdom, resurrection. Such is the productive, generative, generous love of God!

Dear sisters in Christ, Trudy and I want to invite us all now into reflection on these beautiful words of Scripture, these words of life that sustain us and set us free on our shared journey of joy. *Trudy, who are we as daughters of Creation?*

Spoken by Trudy:
In this moment, I am a daughter appreciative of the fact that creation, in this part of the world, is enjoying eighty-degree weather! That's because yesterday morning, there was snow on the ground where I live in Cheyenne, Wyoming. We've had two big spring snowstorms with several inches of wet, heavy snow, and that's a bit much for this Southern California native!

And yet, what a glorious sight to see a fresh blanket of snow quickly melt away in the springtime sun to reveal the grass turning green nearly right before your eyes.

Psalm 104 speaks so beautifully of creation. We hear phrases such as "heavens stretched out like tents," "earth set on a foundation that will never be shaken," "springs gushing forth in the valley, flowing between the hills giving drink to every wild animal," the birds of the air "singing among the branches of their habitation." "Cattle, young lions, mountain goats, the sun and moon, the great wide sea and the cedars of Lebanon!"

We are daughters of creation, created just as beautifully as all of the things we hear in this psalm. If I were to write a psalm celebrating the creation of women, I'd use phrases like . . .

Woman, created alongside man, the same yet different;
    shaped with curves and slopes,
    ordered with a hiddenness to her passion and her birthing.
Woman inherent with a fierceness to protect and a yearning to love
    With a strength that doesn't come from what others assign to her
    but from what she recognizes and claims within herself.
Woman able to co-create with God

and birth nations and dreams and changed lives.

We are daughters of creation, created with the wonder-filled uniqueness of style and purpose as the fullness of creation!

Psalm 104 is very clear, however, about the source of creation. It is God. God stretched the heavens, set the earth on its foundations, and all the rest, and so it is that God created woman.

If we are daughters of creation, then we are daughters of God. Not daughters of our parents, or our hometown, or our society. We are not daughters of our husbands, boyfriends, or partners and we are not daughters of the hundreds of members of our congregations, as much as they might like to call us so. We are not daughters of our staff-parish relations committee, or the cabinet (a conference body of clergy supervisors), and not even the bishop.

We are daughters of the Creator God, which means that we will use our uniqueness to serve God. We will trust that God will hold our lives in God's being and we will hold out our hands and God will fill them with good things. We will sing praise to our God while we have being and we will join with all of creation to ensure that the glory of the Lord endures forever. *Patricia, who are we as daughters of wisdom?*

Spoken by Patricia:

Many of you may remember the huge brouhaha that arose after "The Re-Imagining Conference" twenty-some years ago. That beautiful gathering of church women lifted up images of the wisdom of God, Sophia, throughout the worship of that event. While we were denounced by some as "goddess-worshippers" and other crazy names, we who had been present knew that we were simply diving deep into some of the rich images and metaphors of our Christian faith.

But my Southern Baptist Aunt Ima got wind of this and knew that I had been a participant. She called my mother, worried for my soul. When Mom replied that I'd said that "Sophia" was in the Bible, Aunt Ima, who knew her Bible by heart, said she'd never heard of it. Mom called me, requesting chapter and verse. But even before she could call back, Aunt Ima called her to say that she had researched her Greek concordance and found Sophia "everywhere in the Bible!"

Indeed, God's Wisdom can be read in the creation, in the beautiful verses from Proverbs, in the prologue to John's Gospel. The Proverbs passage is so beautiful: "Happy are those who find wisdom and those who get understanding, . . . she is more precious than jewels."

But as I read these verses again, in the context of today's remembrance of Kathleen, I was caught up short by the words "Long life is in her right hand; and in her left hand are riches and honor." And I thought, *Kathleen didn't get long life. She wasn't rich in the eyes of the world.* And then I realized, *Of course. It's the paradox at the heart of faith.* Wisdom is not measured by the calendars and monetary systems of this world, is it? A life enriched by wisdom is immeasurable and priceless. It was with God at the beginning and it endures at the heart of God through all eternity. This defines each of us, no matter the length of our life's span, for wisdom is the tree of life to those who lay hold of her.

The depth and beauty and impact of Kathleen's life, of all the sisters who have journeyed this path ahead of us, of each of our lives, comes from grounding ourselves in the wisdom of God—wisdom that is life for our souls so that when we sit down, we will not be afraid, and when we lie down our sleep will be sweet.

Our vocation and call as daughters of wisdom is to give voice to the wisdom within each of us, and among us. This is the priceless gift we receive and we offer back in every opportunity of ministry and service.

Wisdom sets us on what the archbishop of Canterbury has called the "*sophianic* search for a justice which is beautiful, a justice which uncovers what the world fundamentally is; a world of interdependence and interaction, a world in which self-forgetting brings joy, common, shared joy." Daughters of wisdom, we are participants in wisdom's search for justice. We are pastors, priests, prophets, of justice and joy.

Another clergywoman colleague was diagnosed with lymphoma a year ago. She and her husband, a Quaker activist, have dedicated this year "to studying spiritual healing, interviewing cancer survivors and thrivers, and discovering the healing mysteries of healing which God has hidden in the human heart." Between rounds of chemo, they are speaking at local churches and interfaith gatherings, in a dialogue presentation that combines their personal story with the pastoral inspiration of testimonies of healing and also a prophetic challenge to create a new health care system in this country. People along a whole spectrum of political persuasions and perspectives find their hearts and minds open to new possibilities of hope.

This dear Kathleen is yet another powerful example of the pastors/priest/prophets we are called to be as "daughters of wisdom." We are daughters of wisdom and participants in wisdom's search for justice, the creating wisdom of God that brings forth life in the beginning and offers that resurrecting "big surprise" when we cross the threshold to life eternal.

Trudy, who are we as daughters of the resurrection and sisters of Mary Magdalene?

Spoken by Trudy:

We *are* sisters of Mary Magdalene, the one who proclaimed the miracle of the resurrection. Mary Magdalene is one who took hold of wisdom, of the tree of life, who was created uniquely for the purpose of God. She is one who took hold of the risen Christ and would not let go. Mary Magdalene is all of these things, and just in case we needed another example of how the wisdom of God is folly to the world, she is that too.

Isn't that how many thought of Mary? Foolish but saved. Diseased but healed. Sinful but redeemed. Not a disciple, but the one at the tomb. Mary Magdalene is so misunderstood by all of us, isn't she? I suppose it is human nature to try to fill in the blanks when the story is sparse. Why must we fill them in with negative suspicions? Mary's story is sparse and we've tried to fill in the blanks. Mary Magdalene? The woman with the multitude of demons, right? The woman caught in adultery? The woman wasteful of the costly perfume? The woman not counted as a disciple.

I wonder if Mary Magdalene was ever criticized for not wearing pantyhose with her pumps, or for her latest hairstyle and color. I wonder if Mary Magdalene was told not to worry; she'll find a man to take care of her someday; or that she could go into the ministry as long as her children are taken care of. Do you suppose Mary Magdalene was encouraged to organize the women's rummage sale rather than proclaim the good news? Yes, we are sisters of Mary Magdalene, and God's wisdom is folly to the world, for God chose Mary Magdalene.

We don't know much about Mary Magdalene's story. But we do know that all four gospels agree. Mary Magdalene was at the tomb. Mary Magdalene was the first one to whom the risen Christ appeared. Mary Magdalene was the one Christ told to "tell the others."

We are sisters of Mary Magdalene, called and chosen by God to speak, even though our voices are too high pitched, to boldly proclaim even if it might not be ladylike, to shout, even, for the good news must be heard, and to keep speaking and proclaiming and shouting because we are daughters of the Resurrection!

As such we claim a creation more just, a wisdom more lasting, a hope more expansive, a dream more transformative, and a power much stronger than the evil in the world. We claim a place in the movement of God.

Claim the uniqueness of your creation. Claim the gift of God's wisdom within and claim the hope of the resurrection. If you would do so, you are invited to come forward to light a candle.

Mary Magdalene's voice was just one voice. Her faith just one witness. Her flame just a single flicker. But it grew. Her voice, her faith, her fire spread to light the world! So, too, may ours. Watch the light grow as we stand together.

Questions for Reflection

This section is intentionally addressed to preachers. Others may wish to answer the questions from the perspective of your own leadership roles.

1. Try writing or journaling on your own creative process for weekly worship preparation. Do you have a rhythm or method for the preparation for preaching? How is it like or unlike these clergywomen in their stories above? How has your worship leadership and preaching grown or changed during your ministry? How do you prepare mentally, physically, and spiritually to lead worship?
2. What is your worship leadership and preaching style, and how is it effective? What are you most glad about in your worship leadership? What would you like to change?
3. One author commented that at one time she became "a little bored with my own preaching." Have you ever had "dry" periods? How have you emerged from times of "preacher's block"?
4. Have you ever preached a dialogue sermon? If so, what was its message? How did Trudy and Patricia's sermon speak to you?

Chapter 4
The Art of Conflict Management

Editor's Note
Lead women pastors understand that learning to manage conflict is a process that often taxes them to the core and requires their most profound leadership skills of listening, patience, and leading change. While not carelessly avoiding conflict, the lead women pastors in our project reported less major conflict in their congregations in a two-year period than their male counterparts (which may be contrary to the stereotype that churches with women leaders will be fraught with conflict). The women pastors recognize that conflict is sometimes the bridge to change, though according to our data, they prefer to lead change gradually by "planting seeds" rather than by head-on challenge. These reflections from two clergywomen provide wisdom.

Making It Work
I was the lead pastor of a large congregation that had been through some very difficult times. I followed a pastor who had been charged, tried, and defrocked due to clergy misconduct. The trust of the pastoral office had been broken. Since I was now in that office, the congregation did not trust me, and that came out in very hurtful ways. While the logic of the situation suggested that the conflict was less about me than it was the previous pastor, my heart only heard the hurtful things directed at me.

I realized I had not been shielding my daughters from my pain and struggle when my youngest daughter, while shopping one day, pointed out a mug with decorative writing on it. She said, "That's you, Mom." I read the words on the mug. "Women are like tea bags. You don't know how strong they are until they are in hot water."

Many times I felt I could not handle the barbs and, more righteously, felt I *should not* have to handle them. I found myself thrown into a deeper aspect of my call to be pastor and lead God's people. As such I had to put aside my "self" and see a much bigger picture, of which I was a small part. I had to put aside my natural inclination to define myself in terms of the people with whom I was in relationship and to define myself in terms of who God was asking me to be in relation to people who didn't want anything to do with me. I had many moments when I sounded like Job, when I fell to my knees in weakness and asked, "When will it be over?" The answer always came back for me to trust that God was working even when I couldn't see evidence of it, and for me to just do what was necessary for today. Don't look back at the pain of yesterday. Don't look ahead projecting more pain on tomorrow. Just be steady.

I did not know it at the time, but that was the key to dealing with this particular conflict: steadfastness. The church needed to know that I was who I said I was, which meant I had to articulate who I was, why I did the things I did, and that I was not going anywhere. I needed to prove myself trustworthy and to show that God could be trusted. The conflict stayed underground for the first two and a half years. Year three exploded. Years four and five dealt with the fallout. By year six, we all began to relax and trust each other. By the time I left, the congregation and I loved each other authentically and deeply.

Not all conflict in churches is about clergy misconduct, but the lessons I learned here have helped in a variety of other situations. Rarely are the surface issues the whole story. Rarely is the anger directed at the appropriate target. Rarely is it personal. Be patient and listen, discern, and ask a lot of questions. Be truly interested and open to what you hear. Remember that everyone involved in a conflict thinks their opinion is important and their position about an issue must be honored. There is always common ground. The trick is to find it, name it, share it, affirm it, and build on it. Always come back to the common ground that all can agree on. It may begin as the most basic of assertions, but it will become a cadre of statements that is inclusive of all and provides solutions.

Most of all, your commitments to one another—even if the pastoral assignment was initiated by the bishop and the church and pastor had to respect that decision, even if it isn't a commitment either of you want to uphold—can become a covenant that proclaims, "We're together! No matter what." And doesn't that mirror the covenant God has with us?

When Stuff Happens . . .

Recently, I was a part of a team interviewing a young female candidate for ministry. She responded to a question about leadership by saying, "I hate conflict." Like her, I was a first-career clergywoman, and her comment prompted in me some reflection about whether I could have made that statement during the same stage of my call to ministry. I'm not sure that those words have ever come out of my mouth. Now, the words "I love conflict" have also not come out of my mouth. But I have always believed that conflict is a necessary part of growth and change, and I certainly believe our God calls us to growth and change. My experience over eighteen years of ministry teaches me that one of my most important roles as a pastor is that of conflict manager. I see that role not as administrative, but as relational.

In some ways, conflict has played a significant role in shaping me as a clergyperson. When I was transitioning from high school to college, my home congregation became embroiled in conflict over a pastoral appointment. As I engaged the conflict from afar, and also watched the community that I loved deeply begin to be torn apart, I found myself disillusioned by the church. Manipulation and vicious rumors could not be the hallmark of the Christian community. There must be other ways, holier ways, to disagree.

As I began to explore and respond to my calling in the subsequent months and years, I quickly became attracted to models of leadership that sought to embrace conflict in healthy ways. I have a collaborative leadership style and enjoy identifying and recognizing conflict and helping communities to work through it and come to healthy resolution. As I look back over the conflicts that have emerged during my ministry, I am aware that my primary role as a leader has not been to create or confront conflict, but to manage it. We don't have to look for conflicts in Christian community—they are present everywhere. What effective leaders need to do is be able to manage the conflicts they discover in ways that help communities move forward into God's future.

As I think about the conflicts I have encountered, many of them have at their root a resistance to change on the part of individuals and congregations. I believe that it is critical at this point in the life of Protestant congregations in the United States for clergy to be clear that change is necessary if we are to be effective in continuing to reach people for Jesus Christ. More than a decade ago, I was leading an effort to reach an unchurched demographic in the neighborhood of the congregation I was serving. As we moved through an advertising campaign for a new worship service, some established members of the congregation reacted violently to messages that were targeted at a new audience, an audience very different from them. In the midst of that conflict we had to be very clear about who Jesus was calling us to reach, and what we needed to do to reach them. When we were not able to maintain that clarity, conflict escalated in unhealthy ways and the changes did not happen. From that experience I learned the importance of gaining as much clarity as possible about my beliefs before entering into a potentially conflicted situation.

Another aspect of managing conflict that I have encountered repeatedly is how important it is for the pastoral leaders to be able to recognize toxic forces in the church system and be able to stand up to the toxicity. Most often I observe this toxic behavior taking place when one or two laity have controlled the church by using finances as a threat, or by behaving in bullying ways that people hesitate to confront. As I have addressed those kinds of behaviors over the course of my career, it has taken a willingness to name people's behavior for them, and state clearly that it is not acceptable in the church community. Often, their response to that is to withdraw, or in some cases leave, usually very angry with me in either circumstance. I have worked to remain clear that their anger is not really directed at me, but often at much deeper spiritual and emotional struggles, such as change or the loss of power. As I have been willing to step forward and be clear about appropriate and inappropriate kinds of behavior within the covenant community, I discover that others will follow my lead.

I've found several tools that help me manage conflict as a leader. The first is the ability to name the system dynamics at play, especially the triangulation. When it appears that I am the object of conflict, observing the triangles helps me to understand that I am usually not really the object, but the convenient person to scapegoat. Once I can stand back and observe that dynamic in the system, I am better able to function, as I remember that it's not about me.

I remember a particular process that we took in the congregation where we were making some changes to the way Holy Communion was celebrated. After some education of the worship committee about the theology behind a common cup, we made a decision to move to communion by intinction, or dipping the bread into the cup. One woman was very upset by the decision, and stood up during the announcements in worship to let everyone know how upset she was. As I worked with her over the next few months, I began to draw some boundaries around appropriate behavior within the church community (i.e., worship is not the time to lodge a verbal complaint with church leaders). I also had to begin making sure a third party was present for our conversations, so that things I said would not be manipulated in the retelling. The more I worked with my sister in Christ, the more I discovered that her pain was not about a change in the method of communion. It was more wrapped up in unresolved grief over some losses in recent years, combined with a resistance to the changes she saw in the community around her. I continued to be clear that bitterness and anger are not weapons to be used in the Christian community, and I trusted the Holy Spirit to work in her heart to bring her healing and reconciliation.

Listening has also been a critical tool for me, and it was not one I thought I possessed as I entered ministry. I have found that when I can sit down, face-to-face, with people who are disagreeing with me or with the direction of the church, and really listen to their story, we can begin to move forward. It isn't that in those moments conflict disappears, but relationship begins. When relationship begins, we are able to reshape our conversation not around our differences, but around our commonalities.

As we have entered a more technological age of ministry, like many people I have come to rely on different modes of communication. However, I have learned that in a highly conflicted relationship or situation, there is no substitute for face-to-face conversation. E-mail and social media are not a substitute for honest conversation grounded in prayer. I always try to invite those kinds of moments into conflicted situations—and sometimes people take me up on the invitation.

I have also had to teach communities that the job of Christians is not to make everyone happy. Jesus certainly did not do that in his ministry, and we should not expect it of ourselves. In endeavoring to be nice to everyone, we have failed to be clear about our mission and ministry and have tried to be too many things to too many people. Sometimes decisions are made and directions are set that not everyone agrees with. We can listen to those who do not agree, and prayerfully consider their concerns, but ultimately leaders need to have the courage to make the best possible decisions and move forward.

Questions for Reflection

1. When have you found yourself embroiled in a conflict that seemed to exist before you even set foot in the door? How did you navigate it? When have you gotten it right in the midst of conflict, and when have you gotten it wrong? What did you learn from both experiences?
2. How do you remain steadfast and make it work even in the midst of very challenging situations? When might this not be the best tack to take?

3. When have you experienced negative triangulation in your leadership, and how did you "de-triangle" or manage the relational dynamics?

4. One of our contributors says that at its root most conflict is a resistance to change. Do you agree? Why or why not? Provide examples from your own leadership.

5. How do you lead change? Describe a particular change that you were involved in bringing about. How did you collaborate with others? Describe the process and the pitfalls.

CHAPTER 5
RESOURCE MANAGEMENT—STAFFING AND FINANCES

Editor's Note

Many of the women pastors in our project expressed that their leadership skills in the area of financial management has increased with experience. However, more male clergy reported a high confidence level with finances. The clergywomen have to face down stereotypes about women's abilities in this area. In her contribution one lead woman pastor shares her emphasis on finances as theological statements. Although most clergy do not bring a background in financial management, this LWP came to ministry from a career in business, and while she insists that it isn't necessary, it did help her to buck some stereotypes. Clergywomen in our study often work with and empower laypeople in focusing on good stewardship practices. Another writer shares about being able to converse in the language of finance, while calling people to also speak the language of faith. A third lead woman pastor writes about staffing and synergistic team ministry.

Bucking the Stereotypes

"This woman they're sending us—we mean—what are we going to do? Will she even know how to read a budget or be able to tell us what to do?" That question from an unnamed caller to my colleague in ministry as I was being appointed to his home church made us laugh. He responded, "She won't tell you what to do very often, but if she does you'd better listen. As far as your budget goes? She not only can read your budget; she's going to ask you why it doesn't align with your stated mission." He knows me well and his answers have held true.

I came from a business background before entering ministry, but I want to emphasize that such a background is not necessary to lead a large church. We can all learn basic best practices; what makes it different in the church is our motive. Yet best practices are applicable across the board—and are no easier or harder in one size church than another.

This is the ultimate motive: To know that the church finances are theological statements aligned with God's vision. Giving is first and foremost a spiritual discipline. No pastor should hang her or his head and act embarrassed to lead God's folks in putting God first in every venue—including our wallets. There is a difference between talking about money as, "Give more because we need to pay the light bill!" and the teachings of using the tool of financial resources in ways that reflect our faith. The church's decisions to spend money are as much a theological reflection of the state of the church as the giving of the individual reflects his or her soul.

Each year during the annual stewardship campaign, I get a knot in my gut—especially if I take my eyes off stewardship and begin to worry about bills. The temptation is to default into begging for the budget. I recognize some only give to a budget; what has been the real revelation is how people respond to whole life stewardship. Mission, consistency, and transparency set the boundaries for financial health all year round.

Giving is a spiritual discipline. But getting past the American taboos around money, and raising the standards of the Scripture on how to handle debt, legacy giving, and more makes people nervous. Or even focusing on the teachings of John Wesley—like make all you can, spend all you can, and give all you can away.

Our legitimacy in that conversation is supported by making sure the financial disciplines of the church are finely tuned to the mission God has called us to. For example, an outstanding building is but a whitewashed sepulcher when its upkeep overshadows the mission and ministry: build with care. A stewardship campaign that speaks more about the program's need for money than our need to be faithful givers, unchained from the material madness of our society, fails the spiritual needs of our folks. If we speak with the tongues of angels about reaching new and younger people, but put no resources toward that vision, we are an echoing and empty sanctuary . . . you get my drift. Church and people, ask this of every single financial decision: How does this help us complete our mission and vision in the best way possible?

Consistency in our approach to finances builds trust. Not running the same campaign or doing the same type of stewardship, but consistency in treating financial matters as normal areas of focus for believers. Incorporating best practices of financial health, learning new trends, paying attention to outside factors that may trip up even the most faithful givers puts us all ahead of the game. We evaluate our programs in other areas; so we must with finances. While other "teams" are expected to create measurable goals and plans to support the mission, finance shouldn't get away with saying, "We are only the finance team, and it's not budget time." When we had a three-year emphasis of increasing the spiritual depth of the congregation, the financial team looked at teaching families to enjoy greater financial freedom. What if our church's finance teams helped us in estate planning even if we weren't leaving a nest egg to the church? Perhaps leadership in understanding the global economy or the entanglements of rampant consumerism is possible. By becoming a consistent and trusted resource to the congregation, we help make two things happen. First, we get past the "all they do is ask for money" fallacy, and we help our congregations fulfill faithfulness in all realms of their life.

Who knows what, and when? While consistency contributes to healthy finances, constant transparency can't be left out. Knowing in a narrative style what the congregational goals and dreams are; grasping that a margin allows us to capitalize on the God-sized dreams that develop after the pledge drive is over; hearing honesty about the tough times and how decisions were made—all of this helps to increase the trust level in a congregation. In one church a large undesignated legacy gift came in. With as much transparency as possible, the church let folks know that the gift was not designated and that a time of prayer, conversation, and examining priorities had taken place. With the goal of excellent worship and reaching more and younger people already on minds of the leadership and some of the congregation, the financial decision to use this gift for a multisensory worship project was in line with mission, consistent with the inclusion of the finance team in the loop of prayer and discernment, and transparent to the congregation. Was everyone delighted? No. Was it in line with our best stewardship? Yes.

I'd like to make a brief aside about a different type of transparency. Pastors, know the finances of your church inside and out. If you are afraid or nervous, get over it. I receive a report on pledges and giving several times during the year. Years ago I made that decision, after finding out nominations had appointed a financial chair who gave not one penny to the church! Leadership with integrity and faithfulness is the call of clergy and laity. Discerning leadership for the church, it would be a dereliction of duty to put people in positions of leadership who had not matured in their faith enough to fulfill their membership vows. I don't care if someone gives $100,000 a month or a dollar a week—but consistency in giving is a covenant they've made, and as the church leader I need to help them be accountable to that promise, especially if they are to be leading others. Being prepared for the tough conversations with those who would openly withhold their tithe in protest to various issues may also be necessary. While it may not change a thing, it is consistent with the emphasis that giving is a spiritual matter.

Staffing is often the biggest financial investment a church makes. The human capital is vital. To maximize financial stewardship and missional goals, ideally staffing is done with the next steps in mind—where is the vision leading in this area? With those goals in mind first, issues such as number of hours, rate of pay, area of expertise, and even who will supervise become clearer. Issues of justice in salary equity can also be addressed.

That clarity then protects the human capital. Again, big church or little, we need to make a few things a part of our regular practices. Clear expectations are necessary in our communication, including the expectation that jobs will change and adapt as ministry needs change and adapt (this comes with consistent feedback, including performance evaluations); making sure our paid and volunteer staff have what they need to do their ministry; accountability to maintaining an atmosphere where ideas can and do come from all manner of folks; and an understanding that all of our work is to be done as if we were doing it for God! Careful selection, screening, evaluations, and even letting someone go who is unable or unwilling to do the work are all important. While it may sound odd, one of the most helpful things in hiring conversations is that in working for the church they will need to be able to lose their innocence without losing their faith. Yes, I say that directly to each interviewee for all positions. To look for some kind of monastic escape in the sometimes high-pressure environment of the church office is a career killer.

When the church, clergy, and laity know the mission and stick it as the landing point for all their decisions; when the church consistently and calmly interacts on finances, staffing, or all church activities; and when we are transparent in our work together, then there is a holistic nature to all the sections. Every person and every avenue together create the unique way the local church is making disciples for the transformation of the world.

Bilingual in Faith and Finance

When I was asked to reflect on my experience as a lead pastor in the area of church finance, the very first thing that popped into my head was a quote from Samuel Johnson about women preachers: "Sir, a woman's preaching is like a dog's walking on his hind legs. It is not done well; but you are surprised to find it done at all."[1] I vividly recall walking into the first meeting of the finance committee in my new appointment as their first female lead pastor. There, gathered around the gleaming conference room table, seated in leather upholstered chairs were ten older adult men. All of them! There was not one woman on the committee. (I came to find out that this was the "tradition" of the trustees as well; however, there were two women on that committee, residual members from the building committee. They were not actually on the building committee, which had no women, but had been a part of a subcommittee assigned to "furnishings.") But back to the finance committee, the membership consisted of bankers, financial planners, leading businessmen from the community, and a business professor from the area university.

I sat down and began to listen to the conversations, as one does early in a new appointment, trying to get a sense of the direction, temperament, and mood of the group and hear how they saw their work as a part of the larger functions of the church. That's when it dawned on me what I was not hearing—anything related to the church or its ministry. This group gathered as the "finance committee" was interchangeable with any number of other committees that gathered to talk about the financial life of United Way, the hospital, or the Civitans. Their language flowed with the vocabulary of funding budgets, investments, stock market options, and donor markets. How was I going to be a *pastor* in the midst of this community? Was my role going to be nothing more than a dancing dog?

I went home that night somewhat overwhelmed, and in my prayers I began to lift up the financial life of this congregation. It was then that it hit me—this whole notion of *language*. People in almost any walk of life develop a specialized language. Lawyers, doctors, seminarians, we all have our "special words," which not only carry meaning, but also a kind of power of membership. If you know the language, you can become a part of the club. Language evolves out of the need to express a unique set of experiences and perspectives. Language carries the "culture" of the group. I have lived and breathed the language of the church for more than thirty-five years. It comes naturally to me . . . now. I think theologically because of the scope of my own experience and the investment of my time, study, and focus. It was not always this way. I had to learn and grow into it.

This made me think of being a student of French in high school and college. I worked and worked on vocabulary lists and verb conjugation, but it was not until I got to college and got to know my French teacher (a part of the French resistance in World War II, a student of philosophy, and an all-around fascinating human being) that I really began to *understand* French. It was more than just words; it was history, story, music, culture, art, landscape, and so much more. I remember the first time I dreamed in French, and it was then I knew that I had arrived at a new place in my study. As I grew older and had opportunity to travel to other countries, I tried to keep this thought in mind and always tried to work on having in store at least a taste of the local language. A little bit of Spanish in Mexico City or a few words of Creole in Haiti—they opened doors of relationships even when those words were probably poorly pronounced as they passed through my heavy Southern accent. Even with these limitations, attention to language opened doors of relationship.

As I thought about that group of men around the conference room table and the conversations I heard, I began to reflect on my experience with their language. In my previous appointment, I had walked with the congregation through a major move to purchase property, relocate, and build the first phase of a new building. There's nothing like a $2.5 million building program to learn a new language! For three years, at least a portion of every day was spent either in or thinking about the world of codes, departments, banks, interest rates, and financial campaigns. I learned a lot about the language in that season. Perhaps I wasn't dreaming in finance, but I could at least find my way around the countryside. But this wasn't enough. That group of men around the table had also been children who learned the Lord's Prayer at vacation Bible school. They had memorized John 3:16 with their confirmation class. They were the baptized. Had they forgotten their native tongue?

This question explains why I resonated so strongly with Marcus Borg in his recent book *Speaking Christian.* He wrote,

> *Speaking Christian . . . is in a state of crisis in North America. I suspect the crisis extends to other parts of the world as well, but I write about the cultural terrain I know best. The crisis is twofold. For an increasing number of people, Christianity has become an unfamiliar language. Many people either do not know the words at all or, if they had heard the words, have no idea what they mean.*
>
> *But Christian illiteracy is only the first part of the crisis.*

> *Even more seriously, even for those who think they speak
> "Christian" fluently, the faith itself is often misunderstood
> and distorted by many to whom it is seemingly very familiar.
> They think they are speaking the language as it has always
> been understood, but what they mean by the words and con-
> cepts is so different from what these things have meant
> historically, that they would have trouble communicating
> with the very authors of the past they honor.[2]*

I began to see how I was going to be "pastor" in my finance committee. First, I needed to use the best known language of the group to establish relationships, while at the same time bearing witness to the language of the faith. I identified four goals:

(1) To establish a stewardship committee that would relate to the finance committee and to the congregation. The role of the stewardship committee was to "develop a culture of faithful stewardship of time, talent, and resources." They began their work with a two month long Bible study, and continued to have biblical reflection time as a part of each and every meeting. This group offered classes to help members experience both the language of finance and the language of faith in formational ways. They visited Sunday school classes, wrote articles for the newsletter, and found ways to incorporate healthy, missional stewardship moments into the flow of worship and within the context of business meetings. This group designed and recruited leadership for the stewardship campaigns of the church. They were at times our ESL ("evangelical as second language") class teachers for the entire congregation.

(2) The next goal was to address lay leadership. As in many congregations, the lay leadership committee had defaulted into naming persons to positions of leadership within the church based on their secular employment rather than on their spiritual gifts. My finance committee knew that it had the job of developing a budget and raising and managing the financial resources of the church—they often forgot the "so that," which was that they were commissioned to do these things so that the mission and ministry of the congregation could be strengthened.

Romans 12:6–8 says, "We have gifts that differ according to the grace given to us: prophecy, in proportion to faith; ministry, in ministering; the teacher, in teaching; the exhorter, in exhortation; the giver, in generosity; the leader, in diligence; the compassionate, in cheerfulness." Members of finance committees should be those who are *generous givers,* not just big givers. The committee needs wise encouragers and teachers with servant hearts. They sometimes need members who "speak in tongues" if that means speaking in a way that helps different people fully understand what is going on and why. We began a very intentional process to help every member of the congregation begin to identify their spiritual gifts and to appoint staff church leadership positions based on these gifts.

(3) Another goal was to work on pastoral communication. I began to intentionally consider every sermon, Bible study, article, program offering, and staff meeting as a possibility to teach about Christian discipleship and how faithful giving flows out of a particular understanding of who God is and how God relates to humankind and the world. I might add here that this is also the perspective of our Wesleyan tradition. Helping congregants to connect with the story of their historic church was another piece of that communication.

(4) And lastly, I knew I needed to always look for points of connection. I encouraged the chair of the finance committee to participate in a *Disciple I* Bible study. "I've been a part of this church for more than seventy years," he said with tears in his eyes one evening after a class, "and I never knew who I was." I encouraged him to share some of his insights with the committee and the congregation, and I also tried to always make connections between finance and ministry. Dollars mean opportunities for evangelism, mission, outreach, and care of God's creation and creatures alike.

In my six year tenure, I certainly was not able to address all the complicated problems or issues of this congregation, but when I left, the giving of regular pledgers had almost doubled. The next step was to make more disciples who could enter the joyful life of generous giving. At the very least, when I left, members of the finance committee (men and women) were talking about stewardship and ministry, and I never once had to dance.

Team Discipleship

As part of a clergy couple serving together, I have a built-in team-mate. Most pastors do not, but that should not keep them from working in team ministry with others in their churches. Every church of every size has committed members, many of whom would be pleased to team with their pastor to further the mission of their church. It has been my experience that when followers of Jesus work together as a team, maximizing each other's gifts, Christ's purposes for the church are advanced. For the last thirty years, I have been privileged to serve as a co-pastor along with my husband, each of us in a full-time appointment. My husband and I made the decision together to attend seminary and then to enter the ministry after pursuing other careers. We had not anticipated serving together, but a team internship in seminary revealed that when we work together, we have a real synergism. That is, the effectiveness of our ministry together is far greater than the good that each of us could do separately. Our gifts in ministry are not the same, but they are roughly equivalent and highly complementary. In the local church, we divide responsibilities from preaching to administration to pastoral care equally, and we collaborate on all major decisions (and many minor ones). Since 1980, we have served in three appointments—two declining congregations in an urban core, a larger congregation in a county seat small town, and a multi-site congregation in a growing suburb.

I believe that the Holy Spirit often creates a synergistic effect when the followers of Jesus seek to be in ministry together, and that we, whether as clergy teams or clergy/laity teams, will find our efforts multiplied as we pray, plan, discern, and serve together. Remember that Jesus sent out his disciples in pairs (Mark 6:7; Luke 10:1). He knew that we have a greater chance of effective witness when we are energized, supported, and encouraged by one another. Such a team approach to leadership in the church runs counter to the nineteenth-century vision of the pastor as a "pulpit prince" (no "pulpit princesses" in those days!) or the current understanding of a sole pastor as the "primary vision caster" charting the direction of the church, and instead puts the focus of effectiveness in mission in the context of community.

Certainly the pastor is expected to provide leadership in directing the future mission of the church. But that pastoral leadership role will vary from person to person, and it is a wise pastor who knows his or her gifts and can build teams with complementary gifts. While some pastors have gifts in visioning, others have skills in collaboration and vision implementation. Working in teams allows pastors both to use the unique gifts they have been given, and at the same time call forth and strengthen the discipleship gifts in the churches they serve. Here are a few things I've learned after serving for three decades in team discipleship:

1. Our ministry together needs to be grounded in our mission. A first step my husband and I take in a new appointment is to work with the congregation to clarify their unique mission statement. Although our denomination has a strong mission statement, "to make disciples for Jesus Christ for the transformation of the world," we believe that it is important for each congregation to put that mission in its own context. After all, people support what they help to create, and the local church mission statement gives the congregation investment in furthering its mission.

To create a local church mission statement, we invite a visioning team to prayerfully discern who God is calling our church to be, considering the demographics and needs of the community. Our role as pastors is to bring biblical and ecclesiastical resources, analysis of demographic information, prayerful reflection, and sometimes a suggested direction to the group. We help them explore the pertinent questions and then work with them toward their unique answers. After a period of discernment, the vision team together with the pastor proposes a mission statement to the church council. Once finalized, it is used throughout the life of the church. All ministry areas are expected to show how their work relates back to that mission statement. The current mission statement of our suburban congregation is "to be an open and inviting community of faith through which God grows deeply committed Christians." It has helped our members take seriously their commitment both to reach out to new persons and also to grow deeper in discipleship.

2. Our ministry together should maximize the spiritual gifts of all disciples and help them work together in teams. No one person, whether clergy or laity—paid staff or volunteer—has all the gifts needed to further the ministry of any local church. But each of us does have specific gifts for ministry that, when unleashed by the power of the Spirit, can further Christ's transformative work. That's why in our congregation we work not just with committees, but with clusters of ministry teams. For example, persons commit not to serving on the "missions committee" where they are generalists with a wide range of tasks, but to serve on a specific ministry team of our outreach cluster. Those ministry teams each have a focus—whether it is our food pantry ministry, our Habitat for Humanity participation, or our overseas mission involvement. We currently have fifteen ministry teams in our outreach cluster, and that number can grow or shrink in response to how the Spirit is calling our members to use their gifts. Each ministry team has co-chairs, so that they too can experience the synergistic effect of working together. All program areas of the church (worship, children, youth and adult ministries, Christian care ministry, sports ministry, connection, and education) use this ministry team approach.

3. Our ministry together allows the church to take bold risks for Christ. When pastoral leaders fully team with others in moving toward the vision of the church, people become on fire with the Holy Spirit, and amazing things can happen. Such has been the case in our most recent appointment. In a rapidly growing suburb our church became "multi-site" in 1998 when a smaller, declining United Methodist Church in our community requested a merger with the larger First United Methodist Church. Even with this merger, soon the land-locked larger worship site had reached capacity, and ministries were hampered by lack of space. We invited the congregation to engage in several long-term visioning processes, involving all the constituencies of the church.

After thoroughly studying our community's demographics (young, recreationally oriented population with above-average interest in organized religion), we together decided to step out in faith to purchase land to construct a Christian life center (a gymnasium that would double as a worship space), as God led us to a vision of inviting persons into a transforming relationship with Jesus Christ through sports, fitness, and recreation ministries. We formed a capital campaign team, brought in an outside consultant, and worked hard on our campaign. Then the 2008 economic downturn hit, and the campaign fell short of its goal. As pastors we felt perhaps God was calling us to wait—that now was not the time to pursue the vision. But our lay team, gifted people highly invested in the vision, prayed and felt strongly that the Spirit was calling the church to move ahead in spite of the shortage of funds. So powerful was their witness that we all agreed to the risk of a longer term mortgage debt and in 2009 dedicated our new facility. Today more than four hundred people worship weekly at two services at that site, and health, recreation, and fitness ministries go on daily reaching children through senior citizens. And we are paying down that mortgage debt more quickly than we anticipated. Because we as pastors were willing to follow the Spirit-filled lead of our lay volunteers, our church now has a powerful new setting that is reaching new persons for Christ and welcoming them into the church.

"Synergy" is a relatively modern word for a phenomenon that was prevalent in the early church. Paul spoke of it in his first letter to the Corinthians when he likened the church to a body (1 Corinthians 12). What he said then about the different areas of Christ's church needing each other just like the parts of the body need each other is the key to the success of the church today. And while the leadership of the pastor is always important, it is not our individual gifts or inspiration that matter most, but rather how we weave these gifts together to further Christ's mission in the unique context of each local church.

Questions for Reflection

1. How can pastors address the "entanglements of rampant consumerism" that so affect society and the church in their approach to the financial health of their congregations?
2. One author advocates for transparency in matters of church finance. When have you experienced the lack of transparency in

money issues in ministry, and what were the consequences? What systems are in place in your congregation to avoid fraud or misappropriation?

3. This same lead woman pastor takes the position that pastors should "know the finances of their churches inside out," including pledge and giving information for a variety of reasons. Do you agree and practice this? Why or why not?

4. When have you worked with a church staff where there was a lot of creative synergy? What bold risks were taken and what were the results? What is the role of a leader to create synergy when they work with staff or colleagues?

5. When has staff conflict interfered with your congregation's ministry and well-being (and your own well-being)?

6. The writers suggest some hiring and staff management practices. How would you go about assembling and leading an effective staff?

7. Have you ever sought to learn leadership and management skills, attended training events, conferences? If so, what were these opportunities, how did you find them helpful or not, and what did you learn?

Notes

1. James Boswell, *Life of Johnson,* 1736 (Oxford University Press reprint, 1980).
2. Marcus Borg, *Speaking Christian* (New York: HarperCollins, 2011), 5.

CHAPTER 6
WOMEN AND THE POLITICAL PROCESS

Editor's Note
This chapter includes the reflections from a clergywoman on how she went against family expectations to enter ministry and also navigated the political processes of several churches she has served. Another segment is offered by a lead woman pastor who participated in the process of electing bishops as a candidate in The United Methodist Church. Eleven percent of lead women pastors have been candidates for episcopal leadership, according to our survey conducted in 2010. About 14 percent of active bishops in The United Methodist Church are women as of 2012.

This article is to contemplate how women participate in a political process and what they need to learn about dynamics in a diverse political climate where gender is not the only competing factor anymore. This reflection affirms the finding of the survey in 2010 that 77 percent of lead women pastors had role models for their leadership development and that women "plant a seed" in a discreet way that is more diplomatic, relational, adaptive, and less confrontational compare to male candidates as they participate in a political process.

Stained Glass Windows
"I've decided to change from a master's of theology to a master's of divinity," I said to my mom at the end of my first part-time year in seminary.

"What does that mean?"

"That means that I leave the option open to pursue the elder track."

"You're not going to preach, are you?"

At that moment, I was struck to be talking to the woman who had raised me to be whoever I wanted to be, the woman who had told me that I could achieve anything I aspired to achieve. It gave me pause.

"Well, yes, that means that I would be preaching, Mother."

At that moment, the woman at the other end of the phone—a woman who has always been, to my way of thinking, at least semi-stoic—burst into tears!

"Mother, why are you crying?"

"Because there are many people in this world who do not think that a woman should be filling the pulpit. There are people in my own Presbyterian congregation—a denomination that began ordaining women before the Methodists did—people who, even though you are my daughter and I am a lifelong member of that congregation, would stay home on Sunday if you were coming to be the guest preacher!"

Fearless and confident, I assured my mother that times had changed.

As I left the safe environment of my home church where I had been youth minister, education director, organist, and—finally—associate pastor, I wondered at the recommendations from lay supervisory committee members—mostly men—who advised me to buy a man's robe and not reveal to my new church that I knew how to cook. I did not have to wonder long. My appointment was as associate at a church of three thousand. I was their first full-time female clergy. My senior pastor had been in the church system for a long time, but he, too, was struggling to live with the reality of female clergy. As he looked around the all-male (except for me) staff in preparation for our first staff retreat, he asked me if I would take care of ordering the food. I said that I would be better at another responsibility. He changed the assignments.

Soon, my senior pastor asked me to be the clergy representative on the committee deciding who would run our capital campaign. For weeks, we interviewed potential applicants. One of the two best prepared was a woman. She wore quite a bit of makeup and perfume, but she was very knowledgeable and extremely professional and competent. At the end of the interviews, our committee discussed the applicants. The youngest man there, and a favored and upcoming leader, wanted us to disqualify the "chick" immediately! I could see the only other woman on the committee—an older but very wise and well-traveled woman—rankle. I said it sounded as if we were disqualifying her because she was a woman. Eventually, we decided on another candidate, but from that time on, I made it a point to kindly remind the young man that there was no such thing as a chick! In my heart, I also wished that I could pass on some helpful hints to the woman applicant—hints that had been passed on to me in order to level the playing field of men and women.

The next learning curve came when I joined the large local ministerial alliance. My senior pastor and I attended together. I was the only female pastor there. The women of the host church were serving us lunch. I got up to go to the back and tell the women thank you. They pulled me aside and asked if I were a pastor. When I said yes, they whispered that they thought that was wonderful! The moderator said that he wanted each table to pray for the one who would be bringing Sunday's message. That was me. He came to our table and prayed by name for everyone at the table except me! Our senior pastor was appalled. When the moderator closed the meeting and said that the women would clear the tables, my senior pastor jumped up and said in a very loud voice, "Here, let *me* get that for you!" Then he noisily began to gather the plates and silverware. He had witnessed too much reality in one hour.

Two years later, we were getting ready to start a very large building campaign. That same senior pastor had a massive stroke. Several things happened at once. The senior pastor sent word through his wife that I should carry on without extra help—I could do it! (I had been with him for three and a half years and he had taught me well.) The district superintendent—our only woman superintendent—called to ask if I wanted/needed her help. When I said I could handle it, she said that would be fine. If I needed her, I should call. That was a big encouragement to me. Texas Methodist came by to ask if we were intending to delay our building campaign. We said no. The staff-pastor-parish relations committee chair came by to ask that I assume the role of senior pastor during the interim. He provided affirmation but went on to add that this was only an interim assignment because it would be a good twenty years before this church was able to accept a woman as senior pastor!

That was January, and we were preparing to move on to another appointment, so things were busy. The building campaign was full steam ahead. The plans for our new church included a sanctuary with thirteen large stained glass windows. There was, of course, a committee for stained glass windows. In February, the chair of that committee came by my office. He said they had decided exactly what they were going to put in the windows. The window behind the pulpit would have a rainbow, underscoring our theme of moving to the Promised Land and an accompanying and poignant real-life story. The other twelve windows would have one disciple in each window—one man per window.

I held my breath, and then I said to this wonderful, innocent gentleman, "Let's see. I just filed a report at checkout last month that said 60 percent of our congregation is female and 40 percent is male, and we are going to put a man in each of the twelve windows?"

He sat there stunned for just a moment, and then asked, "Well, do you have any ideas?"

I said, "Yes. There is Ruth, Naomi, Martha, Mary, Rahab, and then there's always Mary, the mother of Jesus."

"Oh, that's right. Well, let me take this back to the drawing board."

The next year, I changed appointments and a new senior pastor was appointed to the Promised Land. One year later, our opening clergy meeting at annual conference was held at the church with the thirteen stained glass windows. As I entered the sanctuary, I looked up at the windows around me. The first one I saw was of Naomi and Ruth, large, strong and colorful, in a field of wheat. Then there were others, men and women, all carefully chosen for a purpose, the women well-represented.

Shortly after my current appointment, the first appointment where I have not been the first woman, and almost ten years to the day from when the staff-pastor-parish chair told me it would be a good twenty years before that church was ready for a woman, I received a call. The caller was part of the leadership team from the church. There was a good possibility that they would be losing their senior pastor at the end of the year. Would I consider taking his place?

The caller did not know that I had just taken a new appointment, an inner-city church quite different from the suburban church with the exception of stained glass windows. I replied that I was excited about my new appointment, and then, after a few moments, reflecting on that church and its future, I said, "I do have a name for you, though, a name of someone who has done a skillful job in the present appointment, a name of someone who has purposefully stayed a bit hidden in order to provide stability to the children at home. Would you like to have *her* name?" The caller said yes. I thought to myself, "No woman has ever had that large a congregation in our conference, and it has been only ten years, but who knows? Maybe they will consider *her*. They should."

My mother now understands that times have changed, and I now realize that there are still many changes to be made. Understanding the political process for women in the clergy and making progress in it requires a delicate balance of patience and perseverance. Thanks be to God for the women and men whose passion guides us in that effort!

A Lead Woman Pastor's Experience in the Episcopacy Process
The process for electing bishops in The United Methodist Church is the work of the jurisdictional conferences. Each jurisdiction has slightly different means by which it tackles this sacred work, even though the same basic process is in place. In the jurisdiction where I belong, the pathway for women to be elected to serve the church in this way has been varied; in some ways, it seems to me (even though the theme of this chapter is women and the political process) that it has been less political and more inspirational. I have

been privileged to be part of that process of electing bishops in our jurisdiction for the past twenty years, first as an alternate delegate, then as a delegate, and finally as a candidate for the episcopacy.

The first woman was elected to the episcopacy in 1988 in my region. She was elected in a groundswell of the Holy Spirit; she was not on the ballot, she was not "running for bishop" (a phrase I loathe). I heard about it from my dad, an alternate delegate that year, who was amazed and a bit frustrated that "the process" wasn't followed. But as a young clergywoman, I rejoiced. How awesome it was that a woman had broken the glass ceiling!

I first met our first woman bishop when I was serving a small town church. She was gracious and welcoming and you could feel the love she had for her sisters in ministry in a palpable way. I have always been touched by her genuine, truth-telling spirit; by her wisdom and strength; and by her ability to relate to a wide variety of people.

Another woman in 1992 was offered by her annual conference in my jurisdiction but was not elected, although she made a favorable showing. She was a long-time friend of mine and my family. I was aware, as an alternate delegate that year, that there was a fair amount of politicizing around the elections. I sat across the aisle from my friend at one point and encouraged her to hang in there. At the 1996 jurisdictional conference, she was elected as the second episcopal candidate. She had been mentored well by the woman bishop I mentioned earlier, a tribute to her gifts and spiritual depths. Again, I was aware of some lobbying going on, mostly by men, who had a history of bartering for votes to get their candidates elected; but as an alternate delegate, I managed to stay out of the fray. Most of the women delegates I talked with were really put off by this politicization of the process, and much more willing to let the Spirit move. This resistance, I believe, has mostly been helpful, but sometimes harmful to the furthering of women's voices in leadership as bishops in our jurisdiction.

In 1996, I joined the cabinet as a district superintendent with a newly elected male bishop. During the first quadrennium of my service as a superintendent, I was asked to help organize a jurisdictional gathering of clergywomen. Our agenda was to meet one another, build relationships, and begin the process of popcorning the names of women who could be possible future episcopal leaders. Two women bishops met with us and encouraged us to hear God's possibilities for our lives. Many names were lifted up at that meeting, and two of them have become bishops since then. My name was also lifted up. It was a humbling experience.

In 2000, at our annual conference session, three names were brought as possible episcopal candidates: a popular and competent white male pastor who had been endorsed the previous year for the episcopacy in our annual conference; a racial-ethnic male candidate, and me, from the clergywomen. The three of us met for prayer and conversation, and at the end of our conversation the white male asked the racial-ethnic male candidate and me for our support first: "If you let me run this time, I'll step aside and support you in the future." We agreed. However, he was not elected that year. Only one bishop was to be elected, and after many ballots, we elected our first racial-ethnic woman bishop in our region!

During the following quadrennium, some of my clergywomen colleagues and I hosted the other women district superintendents and council directors for what would be the last gathering of that configuration. I remember sitting with a clergywoman colleague on the bus on the way to dinner and having a conversation with her about whether she would again offer herself as an episcopal candidate. She said that she had decided not to, as she felt that the interviewing process had been grueling and really awful for her.

During the following quadrennium, the jurisdictional clergywomen met again. Two women bishops from our area and another woman bishop from a different region were with us, and really tried to encourage the clergywomen to get organized and to strategize together about possible episcopal candidates, but there was a lot of resistance from the organizers. Finally, one of the women bishops took the floor and just asked the clergywomen to identify those in their conferences who might be mentioned, and a number of persons were mentioned; but curiously, many men's names were also lifted up, as various clergywomen had been courted by them for support. And so we headed for 2004 Jurisdictional Conference with very little preparation and some women who had really been discouraged in previous attempts to offer themselves for this office.

With the formation of a new annual conference in our region came the establishment of rules on the nomination and election of episcopal candidates. In 2004, my name was lifted up, and I was interviewed by the delegation, as were two male candidates. The delegation chose to only endorse one racial-ethnic male candidate, who was endorsed heartily by the annual conference and was elected early in the balloting at jurisdictional. It was a strange year, because originally there were only to be three openings, and then suddenly there were five because of a couple of unexpected retirements. The only women on the ballot were racial-ethnic women, who unfortunately were not faring well in the interviews. I called two Caucasian women candidates and asked them to meet me for breakfast. I had a sense that there could be a move to elect a white woman, and with suddenly having five openings, it seemed that one of us might be a possibility. We covenanted together to try not to let our names be raised until after the election of a racial-ethnic woman . . . but it became clear that the body would not do that. Finally, some people began to write in one Caucasian woman candidate's name—the very one who had told me on the bus that the process had been so draining for her—and this time she was elected.

In 2008, I entered the process of discernment and again offered myself to the delegation for endorsement, as did a couple other candidates. This time, I was the solely endorsed candidate for the delegation. By the time we came to annual conference, and the time to receive conference endorsement, some members of the conference who were close friends with a particular white man who had not interviewed with the delegation lifted his name.

The annual conference endorsed both him and me as candidates. I invited all of the candidates to join together for dinner the night before the interviews, and we had a chance to meet and greet one another. I felt it would help us to form relationship and not see one another as competitors. For me, the interviewing was a time of joy and privilege to get to share my hopes, dreams, and visions for my beloved church. The balloting was intense, and it ended up as mostly a race between two women, one white and one racial-ethnic candidate, but I was not among them. The clergywomen gathered to try to strategize. The discussion was sometimes passionate and loud, with little consensus following the conversation. The next day, a Caucasian woman was elected.

Although I had fun, and felt I was fulfilling what God had asked of me, I was unclear about whether I would offer myself again as a candidate. My husband, who had been really impressed as he heard me interview (and that's saying something since we had been married for more than thirty-five years at the time), was disheartened by all of the people who greeted me in the hall with, "You were awesome!" and "Well done!" but didn't vote for me when the balloting came.

My parents and in-laws were/are still alive and living near us and the grandchildren were growing up, and I was hesitant to move far away from them and family responsibilities. I was having fun in the local congregation I was serving, and it was not a good time to be thinking about transitioning from that appointment. I did not have spiritual clarity about going forward, and I was hesitant to make the sacrifice that the episcopacy would mean for me and my family. I did not put my name forward when the delegation asked for volunteers this time. The delegation met and interviewed two persons, but chose not to endorse any candidates.

However, the last weekend in April, as the general conference was frantically doing its work, I finally had the time to participate in the Walk to Emmaus program. As I sat at the foot of the cross of Jesus, I heard the voice of Christ say to me, "Who are you to decide what you do with your life? You committed yourself to me all the way; why are you holding this part of yourself back?" I broke down in tears. That week I was scheduled to have breakfast with my bishop, and he encouraged me to listen to the voice of God for my life. I spoke with a young clergywoman I had mentored when I was a superintendent (a member of the delegation), and gave her my permission to lift my name from the conference floor as a candidate, if she still wanted to do that, and she did. I offered my three-minute speech to the conference, and I was endorsed, along with a racial-ethnic male candidate.

This time, as I offered myself, it was with a deeper sense of humility. Even making the journey to the jurisdictional conference was sacrificial, as I had been scheduled to be on Cape Cod camping with my family the week of the session. So I went and a group of diverse people—male and female clergy and laity—agreed to walk with me on this journey. I believe I interviewed well; I was true to myself and my understanding of God and where the church needs to move. I enjoyed the process and had a sense of the presence of God with me. Many are called, but few are chosen; and I was not elected. A Caucasian woman was first elected and I knew that there would not be more than one white woman elected in our very diverse jurisdiction. I withdrew my name.

The next morning, I hopped a plane for Connecticut, where my husband picked me up to join our family gathering. In reflection, I have no regrets. I feel like it was my Abraham moment, a moment when I clearly heard God ask me to walk a journey of faithful-ness—and I did. I, like Abraham, am so very thankful that there was a ram in the bush. My life is back to "normal" now . . . plans and visions of ministry unfolding in a vital congregation, family covenants being upheld, and the joy of giving God the glory in everything!

Is the process political? Yes, holy conferencing could be viewed that way; but the primary goal of holy conferencing is to be Spirit-filled. I do wonder if we would be better served through more holy conferencing together prior to the jurisdictional conference, a prac-tice that has been previously banned in some conferences. There are now some new rules that allow conferences to meet with episcopal candidates from other conferences prior to the regional gathering. This might bode well especially for clergywomen; we'll see.

Questions for Reflection

1. What political realities have surprised you in these stories? How has sexism reared its ugly head in your experience, and how did you respond? When have you gently (or not so gently) instructed

people that their comments or actions offend?

2. Clergywomen sometimes express being drained or disheartened by the politics of the church. Others have been more direct victims of it. What is your experience and how does it impact your life and work?

3. As you read one clergywoman's account of the episcopacy process, and ultimately the end of her journey toward the office of bishop, what are your initial reactions? Do you agree that the process is or can be Spirit-filled? How so? What needs to change?

4. At least one other lead woman pastor who participated in this project did go on to become a bishop. What spiritual gifts and leadership skills are necessary for women to lead and transform the church and society today?

5. Is being a lead woman pastor of a large church a "stepping stone" to the episcopacy? Should women follow conventional steps of hierarchy to succeed? Why or why not?

Editor's Note

The lead women pastors articulated that giving attention to their own spiritual nourishment and growth is vital to their leadership. In order to help others, they agreed that one has to be always in touch with God. Many studies and manuals in leadership do not address spiritual needs, especially women's spirituality, but lead women pastors find that it is the core of their identity and authentic leadership. The following two essays describe some ways that a spiritual maturity fosters effective leadership and how openness to receiving God's grace empowers women.

Spirituality in All Things . . . Especially Cats

In 2006, I was appointed as lead pastor to a congregation with a plan to build a new building three times larger than the original hundred-year-old building. By the time I arrived, the decision had been made, much of the starting funds had been raised, and the contracts had been signed. But the congregation had not developed a unified vision of what their purpose was in initiating this leap to another level of church life. Some envisioned more space so they wouldn't feel so crowded. Some envisioned all the members together in worship at last. Some were enthusiastic about the new opportunities there would be for ministry and mission and worship. Others expected that nothing would change and were dismayed when things did. Some were defiant when their talents or attitudes did not translate well into the new setting.

The pressure of these and many other different expectations of the new building, both positive and negative, came to a head after the move, and there was a split in the church. Now, we are two-thirds of what we were, and we have had to adapt financially, but we are much healthier as a church. We are pulling together and committed to one purpose. We have even developed a "brand" that everyone seems to feel sums up who we are. We are "[Name of Church] . . . at the heart of it all." Our new logo is a heart with a cross dividing it into four different colored shapes representing our envisioned diversity, but our oneness in Christ. As a church, we have become physically, emotionally, and spiritually healthier, but it hasn't been easy. Years ago, I was told by a consultant that the average time a pastor remains at a church after a building program is a year and a half. Now I can see why. But I'm in my fourth year beyond the move, and the future looks bright for this congregation. I know that if I hadn't been spiritually healthy, things might have turned out differently.

I have found that keeping myself spiritually, emotionally, and physically healthy has been essential to helping my church be healthy. When pastors stand spiritually tall and straight through the turmoil of church life, we model confidence in ourselves and in God. When we exhibit grace in the face of personal attacks, we model healthy egos and spiritual maturity. When we discourage criticism of others and encourage helping behavior and an unwavering focus on the Great Commission, we model unselfishness, vision, teamwork, and a spirit of trust that God can make everything work in the end.

Recently, I realized that I hadn't thought much about my spirituality. I'd been too busy! But as I began to think about how my spirituality had helped me through this challenging time, I realized that although I wasn't thinking much about it consciously, it was an ever-present, extremely important part of my steady leadership through this turbulent time.

When I think of someone who is "spiritual," I think of adjectives like pious, devout, holy, mystic, and otherworldly. I picture cloistered nuns praying long hours on their knees in dark, cold stone chapels, separated from the world. I have found that this image doesn't do much for me. I experience my spirituality as totally integrated with everything else in my life, much as the parts of my body are totally integrated. I can't send my left arm to work and leave my right at home in bed. Where one goes, the other has to go, and what affects one, affects the other too. My spirit, mind, and body all have to be working well together for me to be an effective human being, let alone an effective woman pastor of a large congregation.

So, how do we make sure we're functioning at our highest level of spiritual maturity? There are, of course, well-known formal traditional spiritual practices: fasting, personal prayer, meditation, devotional materials, retreats, labyrinth walks, spiritual direction, prayer groups, Scripture reading, and so forth. I've practiced many of these on and off, and I have experienced moments of spiritual depth through some of them. It was at one silent retreat that I became acutely aware that I could no longer resist my calling to ordained ministry. At times, when stress or overwork at the church and at home have depleted us, such practices are especially valuable because they make space that is especially helpful to women, who often try to mother the whole world. These practices force us to slow down physically and mentally, to take some real time for ourselves, and to regroup spiritually.

Having said this, I have found that my most memorable spiritual moments usually happen when I least expect them along my everyday walk through life. The Holy Spirit seems to be most with me when I am wholly present with other people. I have never felt a stronger presence of God than when crying with the parents of a dying newborn or when singing a familiar praise song in a meaningful worship service or when feeling the tension dissipate after someone makes a gesture of reconciliation. I have come to accept that I don't feel any more spiritual when I am sitting alone in a silent room with the Bible and a candle than I do when I'm writing my sermon or visiting the hospital or even when I'm poring over the financial statements or talking on the phone or watching a movie. For me, my spirituality is really about how I approach these things. To this end, I have developed the habit of continually asking myself, "Where is God in this?" And to my continual amazement,

I pretty much see God in everything if I just keep looking.

For example, there is something deeply spiritual for me about the presence of my cat, but the spiritual nature of this is hard to capture in words. It is an experience that exists simply in the moment. If you enjoy cats as I do, you just feel it: the peace, the trust, the lack of anxiety, the gentle rhythm of their breathing, the complete and utter relaxation . . . it's contagious. They say your blood pressure goes down when you pet a cat. And I find it very hard to feel angry or anxious when my cat is chasing her shadow or nuzzling my hand trying to get her chin scratched. I find myself smiling and lost in the moment of pleasure even if it has been the hardest day on record for a lead pastor. Things that are good for us spiritually are likely to also be good for us physically and emotionally, and similarly, what is good for us emotionally or physically is likely good for us spiritually too. Noticing such things and being thankful for them connects us with the gift and godliness of them.

I have worked hard for many years to be as healthy and integrated a person as I can because it helps in every situation I encounter. But it is also a reality of life as a pastor that we are often surrounded by people who are not very healthy at all. It is all too easy even for the healthiest pastor to fall into old patterns of relationship that can be destructive to everyone involved. Going off to the sanctuary to pray and ask God to intervene may seem like the most "spiritual" thing to do, and I certainly do my fair share of lifting my eyes upward in supplication, but I also find that it can be just as spiritual to enter into real and honest relationship with others. It is in many ways a spiritual exercise to work at understanding others, to work with those people who might be able to grow and help them mature one little step at a time, to find ways to work around those who don't want to grow or just aren't ready, and finally, to confront those who are being destructive to the ministries and cooperative "soul" of the church. As strange as it sounds, I often feel at my most spiritual at such times, because I can see God working through me in all these ways.

Finally, although I don't have children myself, I'm convinced that I often use my mothering instincts in leading the church. Good mothers know when to sympathize and when to cajole, when to hold accountable and when to forgive, when to help and when to allow creativity to emerge, when to draw limits and when to set free. I believe that a big part of a woman leader's spirituality is in honoring and trusting those instincts that God has given us.

Leading this church is the most complex thing I've ever done. The experience has lifted me to the highest heights of my ministry and plummeted me to the lowest depths of it as well. But through this wild fluctuation, I have known the security of God's constancy. Each of us finds our own best practices for developing and maintaining a healthy spiritual life, but I am convinced that having a healthy spiritual life is essential to an effective ministry as a lead woman pastor.

Growing in Grace: Developing by Divine Power

My understanding of servant leadership includes five dimensions: (1) collaborating leadership; (2) enabling systemic change; (3) facilitating cohesiveness; (4) executing with integrity; and (5) growing in grace. Though these leadership dimensions are applicable regardless of gender and vocation, I live them out in particular ways as a clergywoman. In this essay I am concentrating on the fifth one, which I believe is also the foundational discipline unique to Christian leadership. That is, we grow in grace as God's divine power works in our lives.

What is grace? John Wesley's order of salvation includes the prevenient, justifying, sanctifying, and glorifying grace of God. This multifaceted definition of grace is one of the best gifts that The United Methodist Church offers the worldwide Christian movement. It presents a reality that when embraced transforms every leader—for that matter, every Christ follower.

Like all people of faith, I have my personal story of how God's grace has changed and shaped my life. This story began earlier than my first memory and continues even today as I continue to grow daily in my walk with Jesus Christ.

I first publicly accepted God's grace in my life as a child during an old-fashioned revival service in a rural church pastored by my dad. Many times I had heard my father preach about the Good News of God's grace. In addition I had seen God's grace at work in the lives of my parents, siblings, extended family, neighbors, and friends on numerous occasions. And God's *prevenient grace* had been working in my life for years prior to that moment, preparing my heart and wooing me into a relationship with Jesus Christ. However, during the revival service that eventful evening I experienced an aspect of God's grace that I did not know previously. Though quite young, I realized that I committed wrong actions and displayed inappropriate attitudes in my daily life. I felt convicted to ask God to forgive me for the sin in my life. When I did, God's powerful *justifying grace* made everything "well with my soul."

Since that moment in time God's *sanctifying grace* has been shaping and changing me daily. As a result I continue to grow in grace every day, continually being transformed little by little by the divine power of God working in and through me.

I anticipate that one day on the other side of heaven I will experience God's *glorifying grace*. I do not have a full grasp of what that will be like. But I am certain that it will be wonderful for all of creation, including Christ-followers!

God is the One who offers us this life-shaping, life-changing grace. Yet, you and I also have a role to play in growing in grace. Our part is to open ourselves to *receive* the grace God offers to us (Phil. 2:12–13). One of the best ways that I have found to do this is by showing up regularly to spend time with God. It sounds like such an ordinary practice. However, this means of grace has an extraordinary effect upon my daily life. This is not surprising—because one cannot spend time in the presence of the living God without experiencing grace. For that matter one cannot be in God's presence regularly without being changed.

It is mind-boggling to think that we can come into God's presence on a daily basis. But that is what happens as we participate in daily prayer time, regular Scripture reading, worship, giving, serving, and other spiritual disciplines. Part of the genius of the early Methodist movement was the emphasis on the methodical observance of habits of personal piety. As the first generation of

Methodists regularly observed spiritual disciplines, they grew in grace.

I have found the same to be true in my life. Over the years as spiritual disciplines have become integrated more and more into my life, I have discovered deeper and deeper dimensions of God's grace.

As God's power works in our lives, we grow in the grace we receive. We also grow in the grace that we *offer*. This does not mean that we fail to hold others accountable or that we lower our standards for Christian living. It does mean that we look for the best in other persons and are grace-filled in how we respond in times of conflict and challenge. We are able to do this because of the deep reservoir of God's grace from which to draw. The parable of the unforgiving servant comes to mind (Matthew 18:21–35). How can we fail to forgive others when God has forgiven us so graciously? How can we be stingy with grace when Jesus, the One we follow, makes it clear that we are to forgive seventy times seven? How can we not offer grace when we have received it so abundantly? We offer grace out of a deep gratitude for the great and merciful love we know in Jesus Christ.

But what does grace have to do with leadership? After all, leadership is a matter of methods, systems, and techniques, right? That is an important aspect of leadership within the context of the church. However it is not all of it. Leadership at its best also requires grace upon grace. Leaders need grace from others, and the people of God need grace from our leaders.

Such leadership starts with justifying grace, which transforms the leader's life. Every transformed leader increases the witness and health of the church. Indeed, transformed leaders are essential to a growing, thriving, healthy church.

The grace principle is central to my own life. My most fundamental identity lies in my relationship with Jesus Christ. Yes, I am a spouse, mother, daughter, sister, friend, clergywoman, and more. But my core relationship, the one that affects every other aspect of who I am, is that of a follower of Jesus Christ. Through Christ, I have experienced God's grace time and again. My experience of God's grace through Jesus shapes how I think about myself and how I relate to other persons. The reality that my life is being transformed by my relationship with Jesus Christ shapes how I lead.

Then, there is the sanctifying grace that grace-filled leaders offer to one another. This is especially true when we are on different sides of questions, whether in issues in a local church, in an annual conference, or in our whole denomination. We can view one another graciously, with vision that is loving enough to understand the other person's point of view, even when it is different, perhaps even polar opposite from ours. The grace with which we relate to each other during stressful times and when in conflict can be a more powerful witness of God living in us than any words we say.

Often I fail to get this right. But when I do, I listen attentively to those whose views and values conflict with mine, waiting for God's word to me in our differences. When I am offering the kind of grace I have received, I refuse to allow differences to result in me making negative judgments about the other person's relationship with God or motives. When I am relating in a grace-filled manner, I remind myself that both the other person and I are "in process" in every way.

That brings us to the matter of glorifying grace. Wesleyan leadership recognizes that numbers matter. They mattered in the parable of the ninety-nine (Luke 15:1–7), and they matter in the life of the church. Yes, glorifying grace knows that one matters, and that ninety-nine matter, because they are all eternal creatures, on the road to experiencing God's glory. We do well to remember that we are more than any social, political, or economic organization; we are an eternal body, the people of God. Basic to all of this justifying, sanctifying, and glorifying grace, as leaders we need to remember that prevenient grace is at work. That is, God has been working in the church, before the most recent general conference, and before the Christmas Conference of long ago; before Aldersgate Street and before the Holy Club at Oxford. God had a stake in the Wesleyan movement before Samuel and Susanna Wesley even knew each other. Our leadership at its best embodies Wesleyan grace, knowing that it begins with the prevenient grace of God. That is grace-filled leadership at its best!

Grace is a profound part of the identity of every Christ-follower. It is also an integral dimension of Christian leadership. We grow in grace and leadership as God's divine power works in and through us.

Questions for Reflection

1. How is your spiritual health tied to your congregational health or workplace? How do you tend to your spiritual health? How do you embody spirituality as a woman of leadership?
2. How do you think prayer and meditation affect leadership? What are some of the practices that keep you spiritually connected?
3. What spiritual healing do you personally need to attend to right now? How do you envision that healing happening?
4. Often we think we must get away from it all to have sabbath time in order to maintain a spiritual connection. How do you live spiritually day-do-day in the midst of the pressure of life?
5. How has God's grace transformed your life? How are you growing in grace at this moment? How do you offer grace to others in your leadership?

CHAPTER 8
WOMEN'S LEADERSHIP AND COACHING

Editor's Note
This chapter contains a story of one clergywoman's experience in a coaching ministry, and a contribution from a remarkable woman who helped train our lead women pastor coaches. According to the Lead Women Pastors Survey, 77 percent of lead women pastors indicated that they developed their leadership style by having role models. Sharon Daloz Parks uses coaching as one of a few effective methods to teach leadership in her book, *Leadership Can Be Taught: A Bold Approach for a Complex World.*[1] Korean American feminist theologian Choi Hee An asserts that understanding God as a friend is unique to women, especially in a patriarchal society.[2] Women's understanding of befriending God enables them to experience non-patriarchal, nonhierarchical, and nonthreatening relationships with the Divine that affirms mutual respect and equality to women.

The editors of *Women, Spirituality and Leadership* say that collaboration is a "fluid process, open to synchronicity, collective wisdom and divine guidance." It is not an "exercise in subtle domination." Old models of mentoring engage a one-way flow of experience and advice from one more experienced person to another, less experienced one. A new paradigm of coaching recognizes that we all have something to learn from everyone, that we all possess wisdom to share, and that we can all grow as leaders when we are in relationships of mutuality and authenticity.[3]

With all this in mind, after two years into the Lead Women Pastors Project, GBHEM developed a coaching ministry among lead women pastors and those who have potential to serve large churches. The focus of developing coaching relationships was to help younger generations of clergywomen develop core competencies that have been identified through the Lead Women Pastors Survey: staying strong in spirituality, being an excellent preacher, developing skills to manage finance and conflicts, navigating through family and career, and most of all being an authentic leader as a woman.

Walking Together Like Mary and Elizabeth

In the biblical story of Mary and Elizabeth, when Mary received the call to bear the holy child, she was only a teenager still growing and seeking her own identity. Though she answered the call by responding, "Here am I, the servant of the Lord" (Luke 1:38), Mary faced many tough challenges: possible doubts from her family and friends, gossip and whispers from people in her village, and sharing the news with her fiancé, Joseph. Mary left to visit her cousin, Elizabeth, who was pregnant with the herald of the Messiah. These two women supported each other throughout their journey of pregnancy and fulfilled the mission they were called to do.

As an Asian American young Christian (I was baptized in 2000), I felt perplexed when I first sensed my call (actually, at the time, I did not fully understand the meaning of the word *call*). All I knew was that I was hungry for the knowledge of God and I had the urge to serve, but could not see anything beyond that point. When I realized that I was called to ordained ministry, a seemingly impossible task for me, I thought of Mary, "How can this be since I am a new Christian? How I wish to have an Elizabeth who understands and can walk with me!"

Though I believe every person wrestles with his or her call at one point or the other, Asian American women carry additional burdens when facing the decision to respond to God's call. Cultural differences, personal identity, self-worth, language ability for some, and roles between family and the public are all so complex in the life of Asian American women. I strongly felt that I wanted to help my sisters in some ways to overcome these barriers I had gone through so that they might respond to their calls with courage and joy!

When I first heard about the United Methodist Racial-Ethnic Clergywomen Alliance and their mission to encourage a "Mary-Elizabeth Mentoring Program," I was excited! This is an answer to what had been my prayer for many years! At the first Asian American Pacific Islanders Clergywomen Association (AAPIC) biennial meeting in 2010, Luke 1:26–46 was our theme lesson. AAPIC sisters from around the country connected and celebrated our rich diversity and embraced the unity! As a follow-up, we began to develop our own "Mary and Elizabeth" ministry. With prayers and extensive research, we have come to believe that the best way to connect our sisters and to maximize each person's potential is through a coaching relationship. With the help of Rev. Dr. HiRho Park from GBHEM, we started a pilot group in 2012 to receive basic coach training.

Coaching is a positive and creative process that inspires people to maximize their personal and professional potential. Life coaches help people to explore new possibilities that get the result they want by bringing out the best in them. Coaching helps people to bridge the gap between where they are in life and ministry and where they want to be. Coaching is highly relational. The coach walks alongside the person being coached to provide encouragement and affirmation, just like Mary and Elizabeth sharing their journeys. Coaching is also a spiritual practice. One of the most valuable lessons I learned as a result of serving as a life coach is letting go of my own agenda so I can focus on the person I am coaching. Through deep listening, the Holy Spirit prompts me to ask powerful questions and enables me to observe how the Spirit moves the persons receiving coaching to expand their vision and evoke thoughts that lead to new possibilities for their lives. Oftentimes, both the coach and the person receiving coaching are led to a much deeper place where they encounter the Divine Spirit. To me, coaching is humbling as well as powerful. Coaching helps to bring the magnificence out of an individual.

This year, I have been able to reach out to people of various ages through coaching. I have coached people in their twenties to set and achieve career goals and build stronger personal relationships with God; people in their mid thirties and forties who are going through transitions in life; people in their late fifties who are dealing with anxieties in daily life and planning their retirement; people in their late seventies who are seeking relationship renewal within a complicated family dynamic; and most humbly, I have coached a few Asian American sisters who are discerning God's call for ministry and who are seeking the next step in their ministries. Through coaching, we are drawn closer to God and to each other. In our shared walk as Mary and Elizabeth, we support each other with love and prayer. We help each other to discover our potentials and new possibilities to achieve our goals. By God's grace, our faith grows stronger than ever.

Due to the positive coaching experience I have had, I encourage all my sisters to give it a try. Develop your leadership potential with coaching. You don't have to be a certified coach, but you can certainly get some basic coach training. The coaching skills you learn will enable you to grow God's kingdom as well as deepen your personal spiritual growth. Three words that describe my coaching experience are *deep*, *powerful*, and *magnificent*. My dear sisters in Christ: whatever ministry settings you may be in, lead with depth; lead with power; lead with magnificence; lead with coaching!

Lead Women Pastors and the Coaching Process
In our present church culture, the diagnosis of the membership decline problem seems to be clergy ineffectiveness. Within this context, coaching is an important empowerment tool for pastors. The underlying philosophy of coaching is that individuals are the experts on their own leadership style. The process is about unearthing that expertise and tapping into one's own inner brilliance. This personally tailored way of deepening leadership capability is the foundational reason that coaching can be so very useful for clergywomen, particularly for lead women pastors.

When exploring ways to resource their ministry and enable membership growth, pastors will often be presented with idealized models for leadership. These paradigms generally come with specific guidelines and strategies that suggest the pastors who engage ministry in some particular way will grow their churches in numbers and vitality. Many of us have seen such models come and go over the years. Though external models certainly have some merit, true effectiveness depends on pastors being in touch with who they are and what they bring to ministry. Lead women pastors tend to be highly self-aware and intuitive about themselves and their communities. The coaching process invites them to set aside external models and to tap into their own creativity. These women are extremely coachable . . . quite able to reach down deep and explore as yet unexplored internal resources. This custom-tailored approach values and calls forth the unique, God-given gifts and graces each woman brings to ministry. Coaching nurtures truly authentic leadership as it builds personal confidence and encourages pastors to lead in ways that best reflect their innate style. Coaching seems to resonate with lead women pastors who, for the most part, have walked the path of professional ministry on their own terms.

Additionally, it is especially helpful for clergywomen trained in coaching to coach other clergywomen. This special partnership allows for a common understanding of the subtlety and nuance inherent in the ways clergywomen experience ministry. But most significantly, it is related to the ongoing reality of sexism. Typically, lead women pastors are aware of the unique and often palpable sexism that infiltrates the church. They seem to be not only comfortable naming the problem, but extremely competent at navigating it. Naming and navigating sexism in a system like the church is complicated business indeed. There is a special power in the partnership of one clergywoman coaching another through that thorny path.

Encouraging lead women pastors to connect with expertly trained and professionally credentialed coaches is a productive strategy for increasing their ministerial effectiveness. Training for clergywomen in basic coaching skills can also be useful as they strive to support one another and develop a strong community. Coaching is a tremendous resource that has the potential of empowering clergywomen to be especially well-equipped to lead the church in profound and innovative ways.

Notes

1. Sharon Daloz Parks, *Leadership Can Be Taught* (Boston: Harvard Business Press, 2005).
2. Hee An Choi, *Korean Women and God: Experiencing God in a Multi-religious Colonial Context* (Maryknoll, NY: Orbis Books, 2005), 98.
3. Kathe Schaaf, Kay Lindahl, Kathleen S. Hurty, and Guo Cheen, *Women, Spirituality and Transformative Leadership: Where Grace Meets Power* (Woodstock, VT: Skylight Paths Pub (November 18, 2011), 9.

CONCLUSION FROM THE EDITORS:
RECOMMENDATIONS FOR THE CHURCH

One thing that is clear from this project and from working with lead women pastors is that they are a tremendous and perhaps under-valued resource for the church. Since most of the women serve large churches later in their careers, and many of them are from the baby boomer generation, these clergywomen may be described by the current designation of "zoomers," a term for baby boomers who, though they are over fifty or sixty, have fantastic energy and passion for life. According to one article, zoomers have acquired the ability to live a longer, healthier, and more adventurous life.[1] They are known to be socially involved in church or a myriad of other activities and to orchestrate a social support system of companions and close friends. They are willing to give back to the community and mentor younger generations. We need to tap this resource for preparing upcoming generations of clergy for leadership in large churches.

Lead women pastors also made some concise recommendations that have been reported in several venues and sent to all districts and are currently being implemented. The office of clergy lifelong learning of the GBHEM continues to support clergy-women's formation at all levels of church process. Here are our recommendations:

- For the district superintendent annual training, there will be a *required* component to facilitate pastoral appointment transitions involving clergywomen and racial-ethnic clergy. This includes intervention for sexism and racism.
- For the district superintendent to offer congregations and the pastor-parish relations committee an orientation prior to receiving a

clergywoman for the first time.
- For all UMC congregations to have a pulpit exchange annually with a clergyperson of different gender or ethnicity.
- The exploration of the possibility of group coaching for clergy-women in general and women pastors of large churches in particular.
- That there be a physical gathering every other year of lead women pastors and potential lead women pastors.
- That GBHEM produce a resource for the development of clergy-women's leadership for the large membership churches.

One thing that we learned by working with lead women pastors is that their spiritual maturity sustains who they are as leaders. Spiritual maturity is found when a person understands that she has a clear purpose in life, defined by relationship to God. Lead women pastors believe that they are called to serve humanity in their roles as large-church pastors. One clergywoman says, "Calling is a burning desire that gives you urgency to do something about it that is imprinted in your heart because of having knowledge of the ministry of Jesus Christ." We observed that the understanding of an authentic self is alive and practiced, therefore empowering the lives of strong leaders. Integrity and wisdom, which stems out of God-spirit connectedness shapes them to be focused path-finders in the midst of discrimination, misunderstanding, and the hardship of balancing family and vocation. These lead women pastors are not so interested in telling horror stories of sexism or rehashing old wounds, but want the church to move forward toward forming gifted women leaders, and they have much to offer toward that goal. We recommend continued networking, coaching, and leadership development opportunities for women, as well as education for the church as more women take the reins.

We believe that the future church should ask such questions as, "What unique theological understandings and practice do these women bring into the evolution of church leadership in a society where gender, cultural, and religious hybridity become more prominent?" Lead women pastors' willingness to advance human life by sharing their experiences and practices in their respective fields of expertise will enhance women's leadership in the church and society.

Notes

1. David Demko, "The Zoomer Generation: Boomer Longevity Traits Launch New Pop Culture of Youthful Aging and Active Retirement," http://redroom.com/member/david-demko/blog/the-zoomer-generation-boomer-longevity-traits-launch-new-pop-culture-of-youthful-aging-and-active-re.

REFLECTION

TRUDY ROBINSON

Oftentimes, in my experience, the declared goals of a project take a backseat to the unexpected outcomes. I am delightfully surprised by the accomplishments that occur beyond the articulated aims. Such was the case with the Lead Women Pastors Project. This project began in September 2008 with the intention of learning more about the women who serve large congregations: how we got here, how we lead, how we are sustained. We learned a lot about each other. The project grew into how we might resource each other and mentor others. The project culminated with a retreat in April 2011. Or so we thought. I suspect it has only just begun, largely because of those unnamed and unexpected outcomes. It's not so surprising that these unexpected outcomes occurred. We should have known. For Jesus declared that whenever two or three gather in his name, he is there. And the Spirit of Christ was behind these surprises. It's also not so surprising that these outcomes were unnamed. The people of God have always had a difficult time of describing how, why, and where the Spirit moves. But the Spirit moved. Let me try to say more.

Our time together was holy. It was not just people attending a meeting. Although we had meetings and tasks got done, none of us was going through the motions, checking off a list. All of us had a sense of doing something important, powerful, and faithful to our place in God's church. There are times when I, and I imagine others, get so bogged down in the tiny details of daily life in a large church that I lose sight of the larger activity of God in the world, pushing, coaxing, and inviting us into a new and better day. Our meetings reminded us of this continual movement of God and it was holy to behold. It was not just people showing up for worship. Of course, we all showed up and we learned new songs and listened to words of Scripture and words of wisdom from our preachers. But more than that, God showed up too.

All of us arrived with a deep desire to be in the presence of God for comfort and healing, for encouragement and the strengthening of our call. Through the new and old songs we sang, through hearing the words of Scripture through a sister's mouth and the wisdom of her interpretation, through the liturgies we said together, and through the prayers we uttered, we were embraced with the overpowering grace of God that filled us with unfettered love that heals, encourages, comforts, and strengthens. God showed up indeed. It was not just that we were people who gathered. We are women. Mothers, daughters, sisters, friends who know how to love and challenge, laugh and cry. We were able to talk to each other, eager to learn from one another, hoping to speak honestly, desiring to be ourselves and be loved because of who we are. Our time together was incarnational time as the Spirit of Christ embodied in these women and reminded us that all of us are loved beyond measure and essential to the work of God in the world. Although we may not have named as the goal of the Lead Women Pastors Project to have God break through our lives yet again in powerful and transformative ways, that's exactly what happened.

Epilogue

Patricia Farris

In 2013, more women will be serving in Congress than ever before, with twenty women in the new Senate. In a recent interview, Senator Barbara Boxer reflected on this new development.[1] She was first elected in the first "Year of the Woman" in 1992. That year, there was an astounding group of six women in the House of Representatives. We may have come a long way, but Senator Boxer insists that we won't really celebrate until we reach a ratio of 50-50.

She said in the interview: "If you step back and look at the arc of history, it's only almost yesterday that women got the right to vote. And 1920 may sound like a really long time ago, but in the arc of our history, it's not. And so, it takes generations." Pointing to a photo in her office of her with her high school class on the steps of the Capitol in 1958, she reflected that none of this had been in her wildest imagination at the time. "It takes a while for progress. But we're in the middle of it now. And I think there's no stopping it."

I listened to that interview on NPR one Sunday morning before heading off to church. In the narthex before worship began, I was talking with one of our acolytes, a girl. I suppose it was the Boxer interview that prompted me to say to her that when I was a girl growing up in church, we couldn't be acolytes. In school we couldn't be AV operators. She, of course, imagined that I was speaking of the Dark Ages. But that was in the 1950s. When I ventured off to seminary in 1974, I had never met an ordained woman. I had heard of *one*, but I had never actually seen her, let alone spoken with her.

That clergywoman, the Reverend Jeanne Audrey Powers, became a mentor and lifelong friend. As some of the writers in our volume reflect, as far as we may have come, many people still encounter us as the first ordained woman they have ever seen or heard. And in many of the congregations we serve, we are still the first woman to pastor large-membership churches. Indeed, as Senator Boxer reminds us, it takes generations.

During those early years, another pioneering clergywoman, the Reverend Nelle Morton, wrote a book entitled *The Journey Is Home*. This collection of essays gave words to what so many of us were then experiencing. We knew we were on a journey. We knew we were a great motley collection of "firsts." We knew that God had called and sent us, and that it was only by the grace of God that we kept going. Or maybe better said, it was by the grace of God and a mighty troop of clergywomen friends and the lay women who felt so empowered by our presence and leadership, and the men who were open to joining the dance.

This new collection of writings reveals again that the journey is still home, for us and for the church. Maybe that shouldn't come as a surprise to people of "The Way." It's just that sometimes we forget about "The Way" and focus on the institution, and in those moments it's easier to see the hurdles and roadblocks and stained glass ceilings than it is to rejoice in the mighty power of God lifting us up and leading us forward into that future God alone can see.

It takes generations. And so we commit to calling and mentoring and encouraging the next and the next. We pledge to never stop telling the story, our stories. We resolve to be true to the leadings and yearnings of the Spirit. We commit ourselves to the peoples and world God so loves. We know it never stops. We know that God is always giving birth to a new future.

Break out the tambourines! With Miriam and the women, we will continue to sing and dance, to pray and serve, to live and love, to preach and teach, to comfort and prod, to witness and to prophesy.

May God be praised and the world transformed.

Notes

1. "It Takes Generations: U.S. Senator Barbara Boxer on the Gender Gap," NPR November 18, 2012.

The LWPP was a comprehensive initiative of continuing education that consisted of online learning, retreats, and the creation of a support network. One of the components of the LWPP was to research lead women pastors' leadership styles.[1] The lead pastors research has been conducted by GBHEM to describe unique ways of how women leading in large church ministry settings compare to men. In the past most understandings of leadership styles have been defined from male perspectives. Surveys were sent to ninety-four lead women pastors and a randomly selected sample of three hundred male lead pastors.[2] The response rate was 50.8 percent.[3]

Age, Race, and Marriage Status of Lead Women Pastors
The average age of lead women pastors (LWP) was fifty-three years old, which is three years younger than lead male pastors (LMP). Although LWP are younger, they are more likely to have served more appointments prior to a large church (see career trajectory below). Of those who completed the survey, 99 percent were Caucasians;[4] 69 percent of lead women pastors are married compared to 99 percent of lead male pastors.

Career Trajectory
According to the survey, LWP are within an average of four appointments and men an average of 3.75 appointments before becoming a lead pastor.[5] Seventy percent of LWP and 68 percent of LMP were ordained between twenty-nine and thirty-nine years of age. One out of five of both LWP and LMP have served as a district superintendent. However, more women have served as a

district superintendent prior to their current appointment.[6] More LWP have served appointments beyond the local church prior to their current appointment.[7] More LWP have been associate pastors prior to becoming an LWP.[8] Less than 10 percent of LWP have served as chairs of the board of ordained ministry or have been an episcopal candidate. More LWP have been candidates for episcopacy in the past than LMP.[9] It appears that a common career trajectory within The United Methodist Church for women is through the denominationally controlled leadership structure of the church. The most frequent experiences of women pastors prior to serving as a lead pastor of a large church have been as associate pastors, district superintendents, and candidates for episcopacy.

It was interesting to learn that seven males and one female became lead pastors in their first appointment. Does this mean that these pastors already had leadership qualities that large churches demand when first entering into ministry? Or does this mean that more Cabinets perceive that males have a higher capability of leading a large church than women? This correlates with the most challenging issues for women in ministry today. In a later part of this report both LWP and LMP agree that the "appointment process" is one of the most challenging issues within the UMC structure.

It was also interesting to find out that one-fourth of LWP and one-third of LMP are second-career clergy who had been teachers, in business, or had military careers. This means that clergy who bring different skills into their ministry may do well in a large church ministry context where previous leadership and teaching skills that deal with diverse opinions and deeper understandings of finances are expected in the large church setting. The church needs to recognize and use skills that second-career clergy bring into ordained ministry, especially in the leadership of large churches. From interview data the perception of clergywomen is that male clergy are more likely to ask for an appointment to a large church. There is reluctance for women to self-identify as a lead pastor. There is a need to challenge clergywomen to recognize and affirm their gifts for serving the large church.

Education

Lead pastors are highly educated. Seventy percent of LWPs and 64 percent of LMP are educated in The United Methodist seminaries; 88 percent of LWP and 84 percent of LMP hold a Doctor of Ministry degree; 10 to 15 percent of all lead pastors have academic doctorates or Ph.D. Lead pastors are high achievers academically. The fact that The United Methodist seminaries have produced the majority of LWP is significant in terms of openness to women in our seminaries and thus valuing and nurturing their gifts in ministry in theological education.

Salaries

Among the respondents, 31 percent of LWP earned $100,000 or more including housing allowances, compared to 18 percent of LMP. According to The Lewis Center for Church Leadership this finding does not match with other reports about clergy salary. The largest of the top one hundred United Methodist Churches are served by males as lead pastors, and the majority of the male respondents for this survey are serving the middle and bottom third of the large churches. A very few LWP are serving the top third of the largest churches, and their average salaries are about 27 percent lower than LMP, which is a significant finding.[10] This means that there is still a glass ceiling for salaries. The church needs to pay attention to this reality in order for women to break even among lead pastors.

Congregational Context

More LWPs are serving in the suburbs of large cities, compared to LMPs serving in mid-size cities and small towns.[11] This has a cultural implication that the suburbs of large cities are more open to women in ministry. A significant finding in this study is that the average membership and worship attendance of churches served by LWPs are higher than the churches served by male respondents. All lead pastors have multiple weekly services, but LWPs were more likely to have more than three services.[12] LWPs also had more full-time staff (ten or more) and some lead pastors reported that they have to supervise more than twenty different staff positions. LWP supervise an average of two more additional staff than LMP. The data show that LWP have more responsibilities than LMP in a similar context.

Unique Leadership Styles and Skills

Lead women pastors described their leadership styles as collaborative, delegatory, open, equipping and said that they do not try to control the agenda of their congregations. Working with a large staff, having great administrative skills, ability to plan in detail, being a visionary leader, and delegation of ministry are unique leadership styles that lead pastors identified. LWP also noted that they have become more directive, confident, and decisive in their leadership styles. It is interesting to know that more LWPs than LMPs had military experience where assertiveness is learned and valued.

Strong Spiritualities

The most important aspect of leadership for both LWPs and LMPs was "to be personally well grounded spirituality."[13] Another was "to shepherd the mission and ministry of the congregation" for LWP and "to equip and empower others for leadership" for LMP. It may be significant or surprising that more LMP reported that they were able to "help lay people discern."

Excellent Preachers

The three greatest gifts for ministry described among LWP are preaching, leadership, and administration. Preaching, teaching, and administration are the top three for LMPs. About half of lead pastors are spending ten or more hours for sermon preparation each week. Being a good preacher is one of the most important qualities of leadership for a lead pastor. Lead pastors spend the majority of their time (more than 70 percent) in worship planning, administration, pastoral care, and meetings.

Strong Financial Management

More than 60 percent of LWP reported that their confidence level with financial management has improved and their skills of managing finance have changed since becoming a LWP. More LWP use indirect communication, through other leaders in the congregation, about stewardship. More LMP feel comfortable talking about money directly. More LWP (49 percent) than LMP (34 percent) reported that they feel confident in fundraising. However, only 33 percent of LWP reported that they feel confident in church finances, compared to 58 percent of LMP.

Conflict Management/Change

LWP reported fewer major conflicts for the last two years than LMP[14] and more LWP considered conflict something to be avoided, according to the survey. For example, more LWP would rather ignore the situation if they are verbally attacked by a parishioner in a meeting. Staff and clergy, changes in worship style, and finances are top conflict sources among lead pastors. More LWP reported conflict with local outreach groups.[15] This may indicate that LWPs are better accepted within United Methodist congregations because of denominational commitments to gender inclusiveness than the surrounding community that have different values and theological understandings about women. More LWP lead change by "informally planting seeds and hope they take root," and LMP are more likely to lead change by "intentionally recruiting support from individuals and groups."[16] More LMP are seeking feedback from the congregation, and more of them perceive that their congregations value a "nurturing" leadership style. They also tend more to make decisions by "analyzing the issues involved" than LWP. This shows that LWP have a less head-on confronting leadership style in terms of conflict management. LWP also appear more discreet in terms of leading changes. They seek others' assistance more than men do in terms of dealing with sensitive issues, such as financial appeal.

The Most Challenging Issues

The two top challenging issues for lead pastors in general are church finances and staffing.[17] The next two issues are work load and time management. When asked the question "What is the most challenging issues for clergywomen?" the majority of LWP identified that "more clergywomen serving large churches" and "balancing ministry and family responsibilities" were the most challenging concerns. The next was "acceptance of leadership styles" and the "appointment process." However, for LMP the "acceptance of leadership styles" and "balancing ministry and family responsibilities" were the top two. In terms of self-care, 34 percent of LMP take all of their vacation compared to 29 percent of LWP. The data indicate that clergywomen are more concerned about advancement of women's leadership in the church than clergymen. This may reveal male clergy's investment in male models of leadership for the large church and fear of or reluctance of women's leadership. Interestingly neither group saw salary equity or retention issues as significant issues for women.

Perceived Gender Differences in Leadership

According to the data both LWP and LMP overwhelmingly noted gender difference with leadership styles with some noted exceptions. The majority noted that many women have to work harder for acceptance and leadership. They also agree that more often, standing authority is given to men. More men did not see leadership differences as significant and more LMP agree that women are more relational and nurturing. This correlates with women being less confrontational and seeking more collegial efforts in terms of dealing with conflicts and financial issues. For example, 10 percent of LMP openly display emotion often, compared to 7 percent of LWP; 54 percent of LWP rarely display emotion openly compared to 46 percent of LMP. It is also interesting that more LMP perceive that their congregations value "nurturing leadership." LMP also think LWP are more relational and nurturing. Does this mean that LMP feel inadequate in certain styles of leadership as lead pastors? Ninety-four percent of LWP and 85 percent of LMP developed their leadership style from their mistakes, learning, and experience. Seventy-seven percent of LWP developed their leadership style by having role models; 61 percent of LWP and 46 percent of LMP reported that they developed their leadership style by formal leadership training. About two-thirds of lead pastors have taken leadership development continuing education courses. The data show that lead pastors do not have a support system that they can readily turn to within the church. However, it is encouraging to know that 77 percent of LWP had role models for their leadership development. Fifty-one percent of LWP took personal mentoring and coaching courses. This provides validity for the development of a coaching program for LWP. In terms of making decisions, LWP are more sensitive to political ramifications of their decisions.[18] Both LWP and LMP make decisions by consensus rather than taking votes. Sixty-one percent of LMP see themselves as decisive compared to 56 percent of LWP.

Conclusion

Through this research, we learned that lead women pastors still serve large churches as pioneers. Ninety percent of women said that they were the first woman pastor serving as a lead pastor in their current appointment. Seventy-five percent of lead women pastors believe that serving a large church is a special call. Their understanding that they've been called by God to serve this particular setting sustains their strength and integrity in the midst of maneuvering their leadership style as women.

Solid spirituality, excellent preaching, and strong financial management skills are trademarks of being an effective lead woman pastor. Their leadership styles appear more collaborative, relational, equipping, diplomatic, discreet, equipping, directive, prophetic, delegatory, confident, decisive, creative, adaptive, compassionate, and less confrontational in conflict than lead men pastors in this study. Even though there is still a glass ceiling that women need to break, knowing that there is only one woman serving the top one hundred of the largest United Methodist Churches as of 2012, the experiences of these lead women pastors will serve as a resource for the formation of younger generations of women leadership for not only the UMC but also our society.

Notes

1. Leadership style was defined as "relatively consistent patterns of interaction that typify leaders as individuals." Alice H. Eagly and Linda L. Carli, *Through the Labyrinth: The Truth About How Women Become Leaders, Center for Public Leadership* (Cambridge: Harvard Business School Press, 2007), 133.
2. Note the increase in lead women pastors since 2004. The Office of Continuing Formation for Ministry identified ninety-four lead women pastors as of October of 2008.
3. Thirty percent (61) of LWP and 70 percent (139) of LMP responded to the survey.
4. There was one Asian and one African American LMP and one African American lead woman pastor.
5. Actually, 49 percent of LWP took five appointments compared to 31 percent for LMP.
6. Twenty percent of LWP were district superintendents compare to 16 percent of LMP.
7. Twenty-two percent of LWP served appointments beyond the local church compared to 7 percent of LMP.
8. Sixteen percent of LWP were associate pastors compared to only 8 percent of LMP.
9. Eleven percent of LWP have been candidates for episcopacy compared to only 6 percent of LMP.
10. Based on a 2007 report, large churches have three levels in the UMC: the small size (1,000–1,272 members), the medium size (1,273–1,809 members), and the large size (1,810 or more members). Among the small size churches women and men serve make comparable salary; women are paid about 2 percent more. Among the medium size large churches men are paid about 4 percent more. Among the large size large churches men receive 27 percent more than women. Lovett H. Weems Jr., Ann A. Michel, Joseph E. Arnold, and Tana Brown, *"Report on*

Lead Pastor Survey Conducted by The General Board of Higher Education and Ministry," Fall 2008, 2.

11. Fifty-one percent of LWP are serving in a suburb of a large city compared to 33 percent of LMP; 27 percent of LWP are serving in a midsize city compared to 35 percent of LMP.

12. Thirty-two percent of LWP have four weekly services compared to 16 percent of LMP.

13. Forty-four percent of LWP and 54 percent of LMP said that "to be personally well grounded spiritually" is the most important aspect in their leadership. Forty-three percent of LWP said that "to shepherd the mission and ministry of the congregation" is the second most important for their leadership. Forty-four percent of LMP said that "to equip and empower others for leadership" is the second most important for their leadership.

14. Twenty-three percent of LWP reported that there have been major conflicts over the past two years, compared to 37 percent of LMP.

15. Fifteen percent of LWP had conflicts with local outreach groups over the past two years compared to 3 percent of LMP; 2 percent of LWP experienced conflicts related to sexual misconduct over the past two years compared to 8 percent of LMP.

16. Fifty-seven percent of LWP often and always informally plant seeds compared to 46 percent of LMP. Seventy-eight percent of LWP often and always intentionally recruit support compared to 91 percent of LMP.

17. Forty-three percent of LWP and 40 percent of LMP agreed that issues related to church finances are the most challenging issues. Forty-nine percent of LWP and 42 percent of LMP agreed that staffing is the second most challenging issue.

18. Thirty-two percent of LWP consider often and always the political ramifications of every decision compared to 29 percent of LMP.

Patti Collett is the lead pastor at Wyoming United Methodist Church near Dover, Delaware. Patti was a piano instructor at Salisbury University before entering the ministry in 1987. She holds the Master of Divinity (M. Div.) degree from Yale Divinity School and has served  churches near Ocean City, Maryland, and in Wilmington, Delaware. She has been on numerous church and community committees and boards including a long-standing involvement with Habitat for Humanity and the Interfaith Resource Center in Wilmington, Delaware.

LeNoir H. Culbertson has been an ordained United Methodist pastor for thirty-five years, serving churches in the Holston and Tennessee annual conferences. She is married to a UM pastor who serves as the director of pastoral services at Vanderbilt Medical Center. They have two  grown sons. LeNoir currently serve as the district superintendent of the Murfreesboro district in the Tennessee Annual Conference.

Patricia M. Daniels is a fourth-generation Florida native born in Pinellas County, on the West Coast of Florida, in 1953. She graduated from the University of South Florida in 1975 and from Duke Divinity School in 1979. She was ordained into the Florida Conference of The  United Methodist Church in 1977, and has served churches in Titusville, Clearwater, Branford, Tallahassee, Chattahoochee, Hudson, and Jupiter. She has been the lead pastor of New Horizon UMC in Southwest Ranches, Florida (in the greater Fort Lauderdale area) since 2007. She is married and has two daughters and one grandchild. Patty likes to walk, cross stitch, and read.

Elizabeth Givens is an ordained elder in the Virginia Conference of The United Methodist Church. A graduate of the University of Virginia and Emory University, Beth has served four local church appointments in the last seventeen years, and is currently the lead pastor at Welborne  UMC in Richmond, VA. Beth is passionate about helping God to make existing congregations relevant and authentic in their communities, and also keeps busy raising two pre-teen daughters.

Patricia Farris has served as senior minister of the First United Methodist Church of Santa Monica since 1998. She serves on the board of trustees of the Claremont School of Theology and the Board of Directors of the Upward Bound House in Santa Monica, founded by  FUMC to provide low-income housing to seniors and to families transitioning out of homelessness. An Arizona native, she loves writing, teaching, and preaching.

Tracy Smith Malone is the district superintendent of the Chicago southern district of the Northern Illinois Conference. She received her BA from North Central College, the MDiv from Garrett-Evangelical and a Doctor of Ministry (DMin) from United Theological Seminary. Tracy has  been a pastor in diverse settings, including Wesley UMC in Aurora, Illinois; Southlawn UMC in Chicago; and most recently as senior pastor at Gary UMC in Wheaton, Illinois. Her leadership in the church spans conference, jurisdictional, and general church roles. She has shared her gifts on the General Board of Church and Society and is currently a board member for General Commission on Religion and Race. She serves on the board of trustees at Garrett-Evangelical Theological Seminary.

Marsha Engle Middleton is an ordained elder in the North Texas Conference of The United Methodist Church, where she serves as senior pastor of First United Methodist Church of the Colony, Texas. She holds a BA in philosophy and religion from Austin College, and MDiv and  DMin degrees from Perkins School of Theology, Southern Methodist University. She is married to Blake, and they have two children, Hannah and Benjamin.

Karen Oliveto is senior pastor of Glide Memorial United Methodist Church in San Francisco. A scholar/activist pastor, she has served in rural and urban parish and campus ministries in New York and California and holds a PhD from Drew University. Karen is an adjunct professor of  United Methodist Studies at Pacific School of Religion as well as adjunct professor in Drew University's Doctor of Ministry program. She is the co-author of *Talking about Homosexuality: A Congregational Resource* (Pilgrim Press).

Constance Youngmi Pak is a Korean American clergywoman serving in a cross-racial/cross-cultural appointment as pastor of the United Methodist Church of Lake Ronkonkoma, Long Island, New York. She earned the MDiv and Master of Theology (ThM) degrees from Prince-  ton Theological Seminary, and the DMin from Wesley Theological Seminary. She has held many leadership positions in The United Methodist Church, including chairperson of the order of elders for the last ten years and the co-chair of the episcopacy committee of the New York Annual Conference. She was an elected delegate to the general conference three times, in 2004, 2008, and 2012, and also was a candidate for the episcopate in 2008 at the Northeastern jurisdictional conference.

HiRho Y. Park is director of clergy lifelong learning for the General Board of Higher Education and Ministry of The United Methodist Church. She gives leadership to professional development and spiritual formation of United Methodist clergy through continuing education. HiRho also provides support and leadership for United Methodist clergywomen and racial-ethnic pastors. She is an ordained elder of the Baltimore-Washington Annual conference and holds a D. Min. degree from Wesley Theological Seminary in Washington, DC, and a Ph.D. from Boston University. She is the innovator of the *online continuing education consortium* and the *UMC Cyber Campus.*

Nancy Rankin currently serves as a district superintendent in the Western North Carolina Conference. She has been the pastor of small to very large churches in her twenty-nine years of ministry. She served for four years as the conference director of congregational development. A graduate of Duke Divinity School, she also did her doctoral work with Dr. Michael Slaughter through United Theological Seminary. Nancy is married and has two children and five grandchildren.

Judith Reedy is an ordained elder who has been in church ministry since 1977, serving large and mid-sized churches in almost every capacity. She and her husband, superintendent of schools in Frisco, Texas, have three adult sons and four grandchildren. Judith is currently serving in an appointment which she thinks is a slice of heaven—diverse, multicultural, reconciling, all-inclusive, and historical—living out the gospel, filled with the Holy Spirit, and in mission to and with the surrounding community.

Trudy Robinson was raised in Southern Califor-
nia and earned a bachelor's degree in art from the
California State University at Fullerton in 1988.
She had her own graphic design company for a
few years before entering seminary. She received
the MDiv degree at the Iliff School of Theology
in 1998. Trudy served the Westminster United Methodist Church
from 1997 to 2001 as youth pastor and then as family life pastor.
She served on the pastoral team at First United Methodist Church
in Loveland from 2001 to 2005. In August 2005, she came to be
among the people of Cheyenne, Wyoming, serving the First United
Methodist Church.

Robin Roderick has served First United
Methodist in St. Charles, Missouri, since 2005 as
the senior pastor. She is the first woman senior
pastor, and at the time of her appointment, it
was the largest church a woman had served in
that capacity. A graduate of St. Paul School of
Theology, she is an elder in the Missouri Conference. Her personal
mission statement is "to create passion for the learning and the living of the Gospel of Jesus Christ."

Sharon L. Vandegrift is executive director and
coach for Bridge-the-Gap Life Coaching Serv-
ices, LLC (www.btglifecoaching.com), and a
clergy member of the Eastern Pennsylvania Conference. She is a life and leadership coach whose
ministry focus is to empower clergywomen to
excel. Having served as campus minister, pastor of small congregations, and head of staff of larger congregations, Sharon has a
special affinity for the work of the professional pastor that makes
her an extremely effective coach for clergywomen.

Debbie Wallace-Padgett was elected a bishop of The United Methodist Church at the 2012 Southeastern Jurisdictional Conference. Over the past thirty years she has also served as pastor, district superintendent and staff team member. In addition she has led in various roles at the conference, jurisdictional, and general church levels. She is married to Rev. Lee Padgett, a deacon in The United Methodist Church. They have two college-aged children, Leanndra and Andrew.

Ingrid Wang was born and raised in Taiwan and so brings a blend of Eastern and Western culture to her ministry. She has an MDiv degree from Wesley Theological Seminary and is one of the co-authors of *Reclaiming the Wesleyan Tradition-John Wesley's Sermons for Today.* Ingrid currently serves as the pastor of the Bethel UMC in Upper Marlboro, Maryland, a developing multi-cultural church in the Baltimore-Washington Conference. At the national level, she serves as the chairperson of the AAPIC, Asian American and Pacific Islander United Methodist Clergywomen Association. She is also a life coach. She has been coaching people of various ages to develop/achieve their career goals, maximize their potential, and strengthen their personal relationships with God. She enjoys traveling, skiing, reading, theater, singing, and dancing.

Martha D. Ward was ordained as an elder in the Iowa Conference in 1981. She is currently a lead co-pastor of Ankeny First United Methodist Church, a 2,600-member multi-site congregation near Des Moines, Iowa. Martha's passions in ministry include worship and preaching and empowering laity to fulfill their callings. Martha holds undergraduate and graduate degrees (education-guidance counseling) from the University of Kansas and received her MDiv from Pacific School of Religion in Berkeley, California, in 1979.

Susan Willhauck is associate professor of pastoral theology at Atlantic School of Theology in Halifax, Nova Scotia. She received the Masters of Theological Studies from Wesley Theological Seminary and the Ph.D. from the Catholic University of America. Prior to teaching at AST she  was on the faculty of Wesley Theological Seminary for eleven years. Susan has also served various United Methodist congregations in the Baltimore, North Georgia, and Virginia conferences. She is co-director of the Lead Women Pastors Project of The United Methodist Church and has published numerous articles and three books, including *The Web of Women's Leadership: Recasting Congregational Ministry* (Abingdon Press) and *Backtalk! Women Leaders Changing the Church* (Pilgrim Press) and *Ministry Unplugged: Uncommon Calls to Serve* (Chalice Press), www.susanwillhauck.com.

CPSIA information can be obtained
at www.ICGtesting.com
Printed in the USA
LVOW11s1729011017
550765LV00002BA/384/P